Young Playwrights' Theater's

2015 New Play Festival

A collection of 32 outstanding new plays written by YPT students ages 8-17

YPT 20 YEARS

Young Playwrights' Theater

Young Playwrights' Theater (YPT) is the only professional theater in Washington, DC dedicated entirely to arts education. By teaching students to express themselves through the art of playwriting, YPT develops students' language skills, and empowers them with the creativity, confidence and critical thinking skills they need to succeed in school and beyond. YPT honors its students by involving them in a high-quality artistic process where they feel simultaneously respected and challenged and by engaging professional theater artists in producing student plays for the community.

Introduction

by YPT Artistic Director Nicole Jost

This book is dedicated to:

Armando Abarca-Salvador, Evan Alston, Ja'Neza Andrews-Washington, Natan Bokretzion, Vanessa Brotsky, Maiya Bryant, Aoife Butler, Dominique Butler, Dania Canales, Emily Deutchman, James Domchick, Rose Duane, Carlos Espinosa, Jaiden Fisher, Jabari Hicks, Vanessa Iglesias, Stefan Ivanoui, Toneisha Johnson, Shannya Judd, Scott Lake, Rachel Masterson, Kaitlyn Murphy, Donnice Robinson, Karla Rodriguez, Aijah T. Royal, Phoebe Snow, Zach Stone, Nanichi Vargas, Arnasia Vaughn, Edward Wade, Anderson Waltz and Kamarian Watkins.

They are the 32 young playwrights, as young as eight and as old as seventeen, who wrote the funny, brave and challenging plays enclosed in the following pages. Many of them had never written a play before.

For twenty years, Young Playwrights' Theater (YPT) has worked to inspire young people to realize the power of their own voices. We teach students to express themselves through the art of playwriting because we believe in the power of creative self-expression. Our programs develop students' language skills and empower them with the creativity, confidence and critical thinking skills they need to succeed in school and beyond.

But we don't stop there. We share our students' plays with the larger community through professional performances with talented adult artists. We honor our students by involving them in a high-quality artistic process where they feel simultaneously respected and challenged, and we invite them to share their perspectives with the public.

Our largest performance by far is the annual *New Play Festival*. The *New Play Festival* is the culmination and celebration of our oldest and largest program, the *In-School Playwriting Program*. We work with students in all eight wards of the District and surrounding counties during twelve-week residencies. The goal of every *In-School* student? To write his or her own original play.

In 2015, students in the *In-School Program* penned over 1,000 brand-new plays. Unsurprisingly, the plays are as delightful and diverse as the students themselves, and every single play was read in a classroom by professional actors during the final week of the *In-School Program*.

Although we wish we could, we can't share all 1,000 plays onstage. Winnowing down the enormous pool of eligible plays is a task that falls to a group of readers – actors, playwrights, directors, designers, teaching artists and YPT alumni. The 32 plays represented in this volume are the Finalists, the top 32 out of 1,000 brand-new student-written works.

Once the Finalists are selected, readers review the plays once again to decide which will be featured in the *New Play Festival*. Only fifteen playwrights received this honor in 2015.

Being selected is just the beginning for Featured Playwrights. Right away, they are paired with professional dramaturges who help them develop their already exceptional plays and create brand-new drafts in time for the first read-through. Featured Playwrights attend rehearsals too, collaborating with YPT's professional artists to ensure that their visions are realized, fielding questions from actors and directors and offering their feedback. After months of preparation, their hard work is rewarded when they see their words come to life onstage. There is nothing quite like watching your own play unfold before your eyes. No matter how old you are, it's an experience you won't soon forget.

I am proud to share with you the work of the Finalists and Featured Playwrights of the 2015 *New Play Festival*. In the pages of this book you'll make a narrow escape with a talking bacon strip (page 23), discover the mystery of the strange creature in a mad scientist's lab (page 75), vote for a snowman who wants to become the Ruler of All Worlds (page 41), run through the woods with a wolf who can grant wishes (page 95), stop the evil Paper Clip Man from destroying the world (page 125) and lead an army with a hero who calls himself Faith (page 155).

Whether you are reading these plays in order to relive the experience of seeing them onstage, or discovering them for the first time, we hope that you will be proud of these evolving writers. It takes great daring to create art, particularly if you are a young person offering up your story for the first time. We believe that all people deserve the opportunity for creative self-expression, and when presented with this opportunity our young playwrights never disappoint.

Your purchase of this book includes a donation to support YPT. I am incredibly grateful for your contribution. As a non-profit organization, we depend on community members like you to continue our work. Your support will help us realize the visions of even more young playwrights in the coming years, and reach even more students in the classroom.

I invite you to learn more about the programs that you've made possible by visiting **www.yptdc.org**. There you'll find all the latest news about YPT, including information about our free performances. You can also subscribe to our e-newsletter, *The YPT Wire*, to get a behind-the-scenes look at our programs and receive our monthly Promising Playwrights feature, profiling exceptional students whom we serve.

To the playwrights: Some of you will go on to write many more plays. Some of you will go on to act in plays, or direct plays, or create wonderful costumes or props or sound designs. Some of you will go on to write other things, novels or essays or poetry, perhaps. And some of you will never write another play again. No matter what path you choose, I hope you know that by writing the play enclosed in this book you have proven yourself brave, intelligent and creative. That the lessons you learned through this process will serve you, no matter what you do. I hope that when you pick up this book in five, ten or twenty years, you feel proud of everything you accomplished.

We can't wait to see what you do next.

Nicole Jost
Artistic Director
Producer, 2015 *New Play Festival*

Table of Contents

i Introduction

Featured Playwrights

Elementary School

1 *Silver Samurai* by Armando Abarca-Salvador

5 *Losxy Docxy* by Evan Alston

9 *The Confusion of Being in the Army* by Ja'Neza Andrews-Washington

13 *Empathy vs. Appetite* by Aoife Butler

19 *The Tiger and the Mouse* by Jabari Hicks

23 *The Bacon's Revenge* by Rachel Masterson

31 *The Trip to the New World* by Aijah T. Royal

Middle School

35 *All the World's a Stage* by Rose Duane

41 *The Ruler of All Worlds* by Vanessa Iglesias

45 *Ayo's Audience* by Kaitlyn Murphy

55 *Mrs. Chang* by Nanichi Vargas

High School

61 *Like Father, Like Son* by Dominique Butler*

71 *Sophia and Ernesto* by Dania Canales*

75 *The New World* by James Domchick

79 *A Nobody!* by Edward Wade

Finalists

Elementary School

91 *Untitled* by Natan Bokretzion

95 *The Adventures of the Amazing Wolf* by Vanessa Brotsky

99 *The Chest of Money* by Stefan Ivanoui

105 *Runny Babbit* by Karla Rodriguez

107 *Eliza's Journey* by Phoebe Snow

111 *The Wicked Witch of the West* by Arnasia Vaughn

115 *Wish for Light* by Anderson Waltz

119 *Untitled* by Kamarian Watkins

Middle School

121 *Untitled* by Maiya Bryant

125 *Untitled* by Emily Deutchman

129 *God Makes a Way* by Jaiden Fisher*

133 *Two Halves* by Shannya Judd

141 *Detention* by Zach Stone

High School

145 *Why Not?* by Carlos Espinosa

151 *Back Bone* by Toniesha Johnson*

155 *The Hero Who Called Himself Faith* by Scott Lake

167 *Somebody to Love* by Donnice Robinson*

173 About YPT

*Plays contain mature content and may not be appropriate for children under thirteen.

Featured Playwrights

Silver Samurai

by Featured Playwright Armando Abarca-Salvador

Characters:
TRAVELER
RED DRAGON
SILVER SAMURAI
TOWNSPEOPLE

SCENE 1:

(The TRAVELER is in the RED DRAGON's cave. She is walking in the cave and she spots the red dragon amulet.)

TRAVELER: What's this? This must be some sort of amulet! How did this amulet get here?

(She pulls the red dragon amulet off of its resting stone. She feels Japan rumbling like an earthquake. She sees the shape of a dragon with huge dragon wings and yellow eyes. The DRAGON's wings spread up and he stands on his two hind legs and starts roaring. The TRAVELER is scared. She hides behind the stone.)

RED DRAGON: _(He feels rage)_ I've been in that amulet for 600 years and now it is time to conquer Japan!

SCENE 2: In the Silver Samurai's home.

SILVER SAMURAI: I am the Silver Samurai, the town guardian. My family has been in the role of guardian for five centuries. My family passed on the story of the Red Dragon. The story began 600 years ago with an old emperor who treated his people badly, and that's why they always ended up losing a war. During the war the emperor was wounded and my great grandfather took his place as leader of Japan. But my great grandfather, an old Samurai, had a way of keeping the emperor alive by using an amulet that had a dragon's life source. The old Samurai put the amulet somewhere safe in a cave, where no one would dare to go. He cast a spell that made anyone who went in the cave see illusions of the Dragon that scared them away. The townspeople are too frightened. I am the Silver Samurai and I have sworn to protect the people. _(SILVER SAMURAI feels Japan rumbling.)_ Something tells me that the amulet has been pulled and the Dragon has been released. I'm going to try and stop the Red Dragon! I'll be right back!

(SILVER SAMURAI runs off to the town.)

SCENE 3:

(SILVER SAMURAI arrives at the town. The TOWNSPEOPLE are frightened and amazed! They are running around screaming because they are frightened. SILVER SAMURAI runs into the middle of town and draws his sword.)

SILVER SAMURAI: Go for cover! I don't want anybody to get hurt.

TOWNSPEOPLE: Yes sir!

(The TOWNSPEOPLE run away and hide.)

SILVER SAMURAI: _(To the DRAGON)_ How did you escape?

RED DRAGON: Roar!!!!!!!!!! I was released somehow. And now I am ready to cause destruction.

(RED DRAGON burns down the sushi bar.)

SILVER SAMURAI: Not the Sushi Bar!

RED DRAGON: Mwahahahah!

SILVER SAMURAI: Come on man! What's next, burning down the rice bar?

(RED DRAGON burns down rice bar.)

RED DRAGON: Thanks for that reminder. Mwahahaha.

SILVER SAMURAI: Come on man! Give me a break!

RED DRAGON: I've been in that amulet for 600 years!

SILVER SAMURAI: I know, but look around you. You caused too much damage to our land. Right people?

(TOWNSPEOPLE pop out of their hiding spots.)

TOWNSPEOPLE: Yeah!

RED DRAGON: Oh. I'll only stop if you destroy the amulet because I want to be an emperor again!

SILVER SAMURAI: You are not going to be emperor again because I'm going to defeat you!

RED DRAGON: You fool!

SILVER SAMURAI: *(Turns to the audience)* Can you believe this dude?

RED DRAGON: I'm offering you a challenge to a battle. I'll see you at the cave, Silver Samurai, unless you are scared to face me. Mwahhaha.

(RED DRAGON flaps his wings and he is lifted off the ground and flies away to his cave.)

SILVER SAMURAI: I'll see you there Red Dragon!

(SILVER SAMURAI runs to the RED DRAGON's cave.)

<u>SCENE 4:</u> *At the cave.*

SILVER SAMURAI: I'm here Red Dragon! Come out from hiding in there!

RED DRAGON: I can't believe you actually showed up.

SILVER SAMURAI: Well, let's see what you've got.

TRAVELER: *(Pops up from hiding)* Take that you evil dragon!

(She throws a little pebble but it doesn't affect RED DRAGON at all.)

RED DRAGON: Oh really? Take this!

(He shoots fire at her. SILVER SAMURAI draws his sword and tries to slash the RED DRAGON, but the RED DRAGON dodges.)

RED DRAGON: Is that all you got?!

SILVER SAMURAI: Nope.

(RED DRAGON breathes fire at SILVER SAMURAI but SILVER SAMURAI dodges it and throws his silver sword at him, but RED DRAGON whaps it back and SILVER SAMURAI catches it. SILVER SAMURAI throws his sword with all his might and hits a rock. The rock hits the RED DRAGON at the top of his head.)

RED DRAGON: Huh? *(WHAP! RED DRAGON falls to the ground.)* ...Mom is that you? But I don't want to go to school! Just 5 more minutes...

SILVER SAMURAI: Bull's eye! *(SILVER SAMURAI then walks over to the TRAVELER.)* May I have the amulet please?

TRAVELER: Okay.

(She hands the amulet to SILVER SAMURAI. SILVER SAMURAI breaks the amulet with his sword as he stabs it right through the middle. The middle is RED DRAGON's life source. RED DRAGON starts to fade.)

RED DRAGON: Oh no! Sadly you win. I will be gone for good. I will not try to conquer Japan anymore.

(Suddenly RED DRAGON can no longer be seen.)

SILVER SAMURAI: That should take care of him. Wooh!

TRAVELER: I'm sorry I released Red Dragon.

SILVER SAMURAI: You better be.

(SILVER SAMURAI walks out of the cave.)

TOWNSPEOPLE: Hooray for Silver Samurai!

(The TOWNSPEOPLE give SILVER SAMURAI his victory ribbon.)

SILVER SAMURAI: Let's all get sushi, on me. I hear they rebuilt the sushi bar.

TOWNSPEOPLE: Yay!

End of Play

Losxy Docxy

by Featured Playwright Evan Alston

Characters:
BREAN
CRISTEAN, Brean's mom
BEAUTY, Brean's younger sister
MELINDA
LOSXY DOCXY
DAD, Brean's dad

SCENE: _Brean's bedroom._

BREAN: I want to meet a girl because I don't have any girls near my house because I live near a mountain. I have one sister, one mother, zero fathers. The reason why I don't have any fathers is that he got snatched by this guy who takes any person with locks. His name is Losxy Docxy. My mom, Cristean, always says that I can't go outside when it's 10:00pm because that's when Losxy comes out. I also have a sister named Beauty who has locks.

(BREAN takes a breath.)

CRISTEAN: _(African voice)_ Brean, come down for dinner. Your sister is already eating her African chicken and African rice. It's almost time to go to bed. But remember, do not go outside when it is 10:00pm because it's even more dangerous because I feel like he's moved closer to the house like, he's moved to our house tree. So please, Brean, do not, I repeat, do not go outside at 10:00pm.

BREAN: _(Getting frustrated)_ But mom, I need to meet a girl besides my sister.

CRISTEAN: But why?

BREAN: I need a girl closer to my age that is nice. I need to go right now because there's a party with all the girls tonight and they're pretty.

CRISTEAN: No buts! _(Starting to cry)_ Brean, please I don't want you getting lost. Because ... because that's what happened to your father. He got captured by Losxy Docxy.

BREAN: But how do you know? _(Getting calmer)_ Are you a god?

CRISTEAN: _(Stops crying)_ No. But I can tell you how I knew he was captured. So what happened was that he went out to get some supplies at 10:20 and forgot that Losxy Docxy was coming to get him and Losxy Docxy got him and all I heard was, "Ahhhh!!!" So I came rushing and all I saw was nobody there but a man that looked like your dad with locks and a top hat. He said, "Taken by Losxy Docxy." And that was it, that was your father.

BREAN: Wow just wow.

BEAUTY: So that's what happened to Daddy.

CRISTEAN: Beauty, go up to your room and you too, Brean. It's time to go to sleep.

(BREAN wakes up and sneaks out while everyone is asleep. At the same time, the audience sees a flashback of LOSXY DOCXY a few hours before.)

LOSXY DOCXY: *(To his captives)* You can have 2 hours of free time but you're still under my control.

BREAN: *(Whispering)* When I go to this party, hopefully I am going to meet a girl there. I feel guilty but I have to do this.

(Later, at the party.)

BREAN: There're a lot of girls at this party. No one I personally like yet.

(BREAN stands quietly in a corner until he sees MELINDA.)

BREAN: Hey, you have my dad's watch who got snatched by Losxy Docxy.

(MELINDA looks confused but then the party is over, so she leaves. BREAN follows her.)

BREAN: You took my dad's watch.

MELINDA: I didn't take it. I found it in the field. It was just lying there when I saw Loxsy Docxy. And the reason why I took it was because I didn't have a clock in my house. And then Losxy Docxy captured me.

(LOSXY DOCXY appears in a nearby tree. BREAN sees him.)

BREAN: You took my FATHERRRRRRRRRRRRRRRRRRRR!

LOSXY DOCXY: Melinda, what are you doing? It's past 2 hours. Go to your prison. *(MELINDA leaves.)* I never took your father.

BREAN: Then prove it!

LOSXY DOCXY: I don't have to prove it.

BREAN: Yes, you do!

(BREAN tries to push the tree down. After awhile, the tree starts to fall.)

LOSXY DOCXY: *(Falling)* The reason why I took people with locks is because I was bald and everybody teased me when I was a kid. I needed their hair!

(Splat! LOSXY DOCXY is knocked out cold. The gates to LOSXY DOCXY's prison open and all the people are free. BREAN sees MELINDA freed and they pull LOSXY DOCXY offstage and put him inside a dungeon until he wakes up.)

BREAN: Hi. I'm sorry that I got mad at you earlier.

MELINDA: It's no trouble. What's your name?

BREAN: Brean. What's your name?

6

MELINDA: Melinda.

BREAN: Is there something wrong with your ankle?

MELINDA: Yes.

BREAN: How did you get hurt?

MELINDA: I was running for freedom from Losxy Docxy and I tripped and sprained my ankle.

BREAN: How far is your house from here?

MELINDA: A lot farther from here.

BREAN: Well since you live far away from here, why don't you just stay over at my house? Let me just ask my parents.

(While he's going to ask, he turns around to open the door. He sees his DAD running.)

BREAN: That's my dad! *(Runs to DAD and gives him a hug.)* Dad!

DAD: Son!

BREAN: Can Melinda stay over?

DAD: Sure!

(CRISTEAN and BEAUTY come out.)

CRISTEAN: Sounds good.

BEAUTY: Another girl!

(BREAN and MELINDA walk off together into the sunset.)

End of Play

The Confusion of Being in the Army

by Featured Playwright Ja'Neza Andrews-Washington

Characters:
QY-FEE
STEPHANIE, Qy-fee's girlfriend
ANDRE, Qy-fee's friend
SERGEANT
BUS DRIVER

(At school graduating. Walking down the hall.)

QY-FEE: *(Exhausted)* Thank GOD we are finally through HIGH SCHOOL!

ANDRE: NO MORE HOMEWORK FINALLY!

STEPHANIE: *(With one eyebrow up)* You know we got college, RIGHT?

ANDRE: Oh yeah, me and Qy-fee are not going to college ... RIGHT QY-FEE? *(Looking like he should say yes.)*

QY-FEE: YEAH... I'm going in the ARMY!

(ANDRE looks surprised and is speechless.)

STEPHANIE: *(In a loud voice)* NO YOU'RE NOT. YOU CAN'T LEAVE ME!

QY-FEE: Well, I'm going to think about it at home. Okay?

STEPHANIE: SURE. Make a good choice.

QY-FEE: *(At home, walking in circles)* What am I going to do? *(Looking confused)* Stephanie doesn't want me to go to the Army. What if I sneak there? NO. I'm going to sign up tomorrow. What will she say? Will she break up with me? I'm going to see what Andre thinks. *(Calling ANDRE)* Hello!

ANDRE: Hello?

QY-FEE: Should I go in the Army or what?

ANDRE: *(Looking surprised)* Are you crazy? NO, you're going to get shot! I was speechless when you told me and Stephanie you were going to be in the Army.

QY-FEE: I know, I know, I know, I just need a little action in my life!

ANDRE: YOU'RE STUPID. BYE.

(Morning time.)

QY-FEE: *(Waking up, yawning)* Well, today's the day. Signing up for the ARMY!

(Driving there. There. QY-FEE is standing at a desk. SERGEANT is sitting, watching him sign the paper.)

QY-FEE: *(Signing paper)* I feel like an Army man.

STEPHANIE: *(Walking in)* What are you doing?

QY-FEE: Signing a paper!

STEPHANIE: *(Shouting loudly)* You said you would think about it!

QY-FEE: I did. I want to be in the Army. Tomorrow I'm leaving.

STEPHANIE: You're a grown man and I'm going to let you go. *(Whispers to the audience)* I want to tell him that I don't want him to leave but I know how much this means to him. Also, I don't want us to fight in front of this Sergeant.

(She turns to the SERGEANT, gives him a big smile and leaves.)

SERGEANT: *(To STEPHANIE as she's leaving)* Hi.

QY-FEE: Thanks!

(Next day, everyone is watching QY-FEE get on the bus.)

QY-FEE: *(Hugging everyone)* Bye!

(He is on the bus leaving.)

STEPHANIE: *(Yelling at the bus)* Wait!

QY-FEE: Hold on driver!

(BUS DRIVER stops, looking confused.)

STEPHANIE: No, you're not leaving. I know I said you can, but I'm scared.

QY-FEE: Of what?

STEPHANIE: You ... getting hurt!

QY-FEE: *(Talking to the audience and walking around a little)* My girlfriend doesn't want me to go. Neither does Andre. Wait, you guys know something? No, she would have told me at the recruitment center. I'm going to tell them I will email them every day and call them. But they might be right. I could get hurt, maybe even die. I'm so confused. What should I do, should I go or stay? *(Looking confused)* They might miss me. I will miss them too. *(To STEPHANIE)* The only reason I'm going is because I need action in my life and I need a job. I graduated high school and can't spend the rest of my life doing nothing.

10

STEPHANIE: Yes, I can understand that.

ANDRE: Yeah, me too.

STEPHANIE: I just... I just imagined us going to college together.

(QY-FEE takes her hand.)

QY-FEE: Yes we are. As soon as I get out of the Army we will all go together.

BUS DRIVER: Are you coming or ain't you?

QY-FEE: *(Still holding her hand)* Do you want me to go?

STEPHANIE: I'm going to trust you.

ANDRE: Me too.

STEPHANIE: Just promise that you will be back.

QY-FEE: I swear.

(He hugs her and gets on the bus.)

QY-FEE: Bye!

(Five weeks later.)

STEPHANIE: YOU'RE BACK!

QY-FEE: YEAH I TOLD YOU! *(Hugging her)* They let me out early because they heard us talking outside of the bus.

STEPHANIE and ANDRE: We missed you!

QY-FEE: I missed you too!

STEPHANIE: Let's go get some ice cream!

QY-FEE: On me!

STEPHANIE: Okay!

(QY-FEE and STEPHANIE exit. ANDRE follows but stops.)

ANDRE: *(To the audience)* Wait! *(He runs back onstage.)* THAT'S THE ENDING OF THIS LOVE STORY. *(To QY-FEE and STEPHANIE)* Wait up you guys! *(He exits.)*

End of Play

Empathy vs. Appetite

by Featured Playwright Aoife Butler

Characters:
SUN
MOON
ANABETH
AMANDA
MOMMY
DADDY
FIRST MINION
SECOND MINION
THIRD MINION
CHICKEN

SCENE 1:

SUN: _(Proper British accent)_ I would like to know why the Moon wants the world to be so bad? Well, I mean I know he does not care about what I think! He enjoys getting on my very last nerve! I love to see happy Earthlings running around! But all he wants is horrible people bowing down to him! Oh, and one more thing – if the Moon gets everyone to be bad I will fade away and never return! But if I get the world to be full of joy, he will be forever gone!

(MOON flies quickly in.)

MOON: _(In a fake nice way)_ Oh, pathetic ball of light. Go get me a human to eat while you go down and I come up! I know you don't want to but if you don't I will most likely torture you!

SUN: I will not let you dig your teeth into the beautiful children of Earth!

MOON: Fine! I'll resist the temptation! But only for tonight. Tomorrow I will be very hungry! And I eat when I want to eat!

(MOON zooms out, causing a gust of wind, blowing the SUN out too.)

SCENE 2: On Earth as the SUN goes down, in a small house where two little girls are playing with their toys. The girls are six._

AMANDA: I wonder when Daddy and Mommy are coming home.

ANABETH: Don't know. They've been in the garden planting for a long time!

(Their MOMMY and DADDY enter wearing dirty clothes from planting all day.)

MOMMY: _(Unbalanced and scared)_ Girls, come here, family meeting in the living room!

(Everyone walks to the living room.)

ANABETH: Are you okay, Mommy?

AMANDA: *(Turns to DADDY, he is pale)* It's not just Mommy, look at Daddy!

DADDY: *(To MOMMY)* Come on, we have to tell them sooner or later.

MOMMY: We hear the Sun is going to break herself into 200,000 pieces. If we don't get a piece we will die!

SCENE 3: At dawn.

(SUN yawns.)

SUN: Today is the day! I will split myself into 200,000 pieces so each little Earthling can have some sun to grow their plants and they won't have to live their lives in darkness. As long as they get a piece of me. *(SUN breaks up into 200,000 mini Suns.)* Now I must send the pieces down to Earth, so if the Moon destroys one piece he will still have 199,999 pieces left to destroy!

SCENE 4: In the MOON's lair.

MOON: *(Speaking to three small alien MINIONS)* Ugh! I have a feeling deep down inside! The Sun has done it! I told you three minions to destroy her before she did it! I know that I kidnapped you and you don't like it but you still have to obey my command!

FIRST MINION: *(Confused)* Huh?

SECOND MINION: You never told us that!

(The THIRD MINION shrugs.)

MOON: Now I'll have to do the job myself! *(He spins around super fast which creates a neon blue ball of power and he throws it towards Earth which makes a big crash and there is a small explosion.)* There! I have destroyed 100,000 pieces! Next month on the full moon, I will destroy the rest of the pieces of Sun!

(MOON flies out.)

SCENE 5: On Earth in ANABETH/AMANDA's house.

ANABETH: Mommy and Daddy said they were going to see the head of the war department, something about dying without the Sun...

AMANDA: What if a war is about to start? What if they bomb our house!

ANABETH: Amanda, trust me! A war is not going to start!

(DADDY bangs the door open.)

DADDY: A war is about to start!

AMANDA: What should we do?

14

DADDY: We should just stay calm! But we have to get you two to safety! *(Thinks for a moment)* The Sun! We have to go to the Sun and ask her to if she can protect you two! Here, I'll find the button to send us up to her.

(He finds a button on the arm of the couch and presses it. Golden dust swirls around them and they appear on the SUN.)

SUN: Hello! What brings you up here on this sunny day?

DADDY: It's not very sunny anymore look down at Earth!

(SUN looks down at Earth and sees bombing everywhere.)

SUN: Oh no! Whatever can we do?

DADDY: Well, we know you split yourself into many pieces but the Moon killed half of them!

AMANDA: Now everyone is fighting for a piece of you!

SUN: Let me guess you want me to protect your daughters?

DADDY: Yes, would you?

SUN: Even though there is a war going on, I will watch over your children!

SCENE 6: *On Earth. War is going on. MOMMY and DADDY are there.*

MOMMY: What if we die here?

DADDY*: (Said while in war)* I know we won't, but if we do the Sun will watch over our children.

MOMMY: Oh no! Run, run, he's coming!

(The MOON thunders through, knocking over houses and crushing people.)

DADDY: AHHHHH!

(He jumps into MOMMY's arms.)

MOON: You'll have no reason to fight anymore! At sunset I shall destroy the rest of the stupid pieces of light! For once I will be full! Mwahahahhaha!

(He shakes the ground then flies back to his place in the sky.)

SCENE 7: *Up in the sky with the Sun.*

ANABETH: Excuse me! Are we gonna be safe here?

SUN: I'm not sure, but sooner or later we'll find out.

AMANDA: Can't you and the Moon just be nice to each other? I mean – you have your differences, but you can just compromise!

ANABETH: The Moon is probably just misunderstood, he just needs what he wants because if he does not get it, won't he die?

SUN: Yes, but if I don't get what I want I will die!

(All of them think. A gust of wind blows them to the left. MOON enters.)

MOON: Aha! There you two nuggets are! Last night I planned to eat you tonight.

SUN: Just listen! The girls told me that you've been capturing humans and making them do your dirty work. You do know that if you keep creating all this chaos, we will shrink, right?

MOON: WHAT? (Both the SUN and the MOON super slowly start shrinking.) I didn't know that! What's happening to me? Fix it now!

ANABETH: That is so cool, he looks like a yoga ball!

AMANDA: Yeah, a very disturbed yoga ball!

(The girls giggle.)

MOON: Have you not eaten a human before? They are really good!

SUN: I absolutely have not! Eww!

AMANDA: Maybe if you are nice to each other you could both get bigger again!

MOON: Stupid kids! The only way to make me big again is to kill the Sun!

ANABETH: You should really understand that killing, eating or torturing anybody is never an option!

(MOON sighs.)

SUN: Well, ummm your face looks nice today...

MOON: Your face is not as good as mine but you're getting there!

SUN: Ugh! My face is perfectly fine isn't it girls?

AMANDA: (Nervously) Uhh– ha ha.

ANABETH: (Trying to be nice) Sure, it's fine.

MOON: You're overprotective about the Earth!

(MOON starts getting bigger.)

16

SUN: You are somewhat good to people.

MOON: Really, you think so? Aww, you're so sweet!

(MOON returns to regular size.)

MOON: Well, thanks!

ANABETH: No problem!

AMANDA: Actually there is a problem!

SUN: The Earth is so horrible now! How could you Moon?

(MOON looks solemnly at Earth.)

MOON: I was mad at you but now I understand that you need a good world so you can survive and I need a bad world to live.

SUN: What are we going to do?

MOON: I don't know what you're going to do but I really want to eat those girls!

ANABETH: Really? Have we taught you nothing?

SCENE 8: On Earth, war still going on.

DADDY: I have to get that piece of sunlight over there by the guard who's asleep. (DADDY walks over to the piece of sunlight but as he is about to grab it the light disappears.) What the? (Pieces of sunlight disappear everywhere.) What is happening?

(SUN, MOON and the two girls glide in, ANABETH riding on MOON and AMANDA riding on SUN.)

MOON: I killed the rest of the Sun hours ago it just took a while to die out.

DADDY: Doesn't that kill the whole Sun?

SUN: Just because he destroys the little pieces of me doesn't mean that he kills all of me. See I'm still here.

AMANDA: They compromised. So the Sun gets good people during the day–

ANABETH: –And the Moon gets bad people at night! AND the Moon said he could go on a diet and only eat people once a week!

AMANDA: They both look so happy when they get what they want!

DADDY: Yeah, they look like two little brats, only caring about what *THEY* want!

(Everybody grumbles.)

AMANDA: Daddy! They do need what they want!

ANABETH: Be respectful!

AMANDA: Use your manners!

(Everyone laughs, except DADDY.)

SUN: Well, what's going to happen now? There is nothing interesting that's going to happen.

MOON: You don't know that for a fact.

(A CHICKEN runs out onstage and starts doing the chicken dance.)

DADDY: There's one thing you guys haven't noticed. War is still going on.

MOON: Not to worry! I can eat everyone, there would–

DADDY, AMANDA, ANABETH, SUN: NOOOOOOOOOOOO!

MOON: Fine, but you don't have to be so mean!

SUN: I'll just do my thing.

ANABETH: As long as 'your thing' doesn't involve eating– I think it will be better if I–

(The SUN starts shooting sunbeams at all of the battles and as soon as it hits them, they hug.)

ANABETH: That'll work too.

MOON: That light was so beautiful! I love you guys very much!

(The MOON starts crying.)

SUN: Come live with me! All of you!

(They all zoom up to the SUN's place in the sky.)

SCENE 9: In a kindergarten class in the future. ANABETH and AMANDA are teachers in their twenties.

AMANDA: And that is the story of the Moon and Sun.

ANABETH: And guess why sunrise and sunset are the prettiest times of the day? Because the Sun and Moon are reunited in the power of love.

(All the kids ooh and ahh.)

End of Play

The Tiger and the Mouse

by Featured Playwright Jabari Hicks

Characters:
TIGER, a tiger
DAD, Tiger's dad. Also a tiger.
EAGLE, an eagle
MOUSE, a mouse

SCENE 1: _At home (the tiger den)._

TIGER: Hi, my name is Mr. Tiger. I'm a boy tiger. My friend just told me that the mouse that one day helped me find my way home is stuck at the top of a tree. Here's the story: when I was a baby tiger I was playing with my friends in a place where we were not supposed to be and my friends left to go home and I wasn't close to my home and didn't know my way back. So I realized I was lost and felt scared because the other animals, cheetahs and stuff, eat little baby tigers. I saw a mouse on the ground and I asked him if he could help me find my way home and the mouse said, "OK," and got me safely to my home, the tiger den. I want to save that same mouse now that he's stuck in a tree and needs my help, but my mom said we don't save mice; we eat mice. My mom has always loved mice, as friends. She even let me bring one over to hang out one day. But, while the friend mouse was over and we were playing tag, my mom was so hungry that she ran behind the mouse, caught it and ate it. And that mouse that my mom ate, that was the brother of the mouse that saved me. Why do we have to eat mice? They are so innocent. My dad never liked mice because they eat my dad's leftover food. But, if someone steals somebody's food they probably didn't know whose food it is, so they just eat it. But, now that I am a no longer a baby tiger and can do stuff on my own, I am going to save the mouse at the top of the tree—the one who helped me find my way home—no matter what my parents say.

(Enter DAD.)

TIGER: Hi Dad. I am going with my friends.

DAD: No you're not, I overheard you and your friends talking and I know you are planning to save the mouse at the top of the tree.

TIGER: Yes; I am going to save the mouse and you're not going to stop me.

DAD: Yes I am! Son, why are you not like other tigers? Other tigers eat mice and you do not.

TIGER: Well, that same mouse that is stuck on the top of the tree: when I was young, I was lost one day and he was the one who helped me find my way home.

DAD: It does not matter. You're still supposed to eat mice because you eat meat.

TIGER: But, mice do not do anything to tigers. Mice only look for food to eat. And there is nothing wrong with that.

DAD: Well, I am going to roar to the eagle to fly to the top of the tree and eat the mouse before you can even climb it!

19

TIGER: I am faster than that eagle.

DAD: Well, an eagle can get to the top of the tree quicker, because he already lives in the tree that the mouse is in.

TIGER: Well, actually he is not in the tree, he is right behind you.

(EAGLE pops up from a hidden place. DAD is surprised.)

TIGER: Well, if I get there before the eagle I will save the mouse and run away with it to someplace where no one can find me.

(TIGER takes off. DAD doesn't see this.)

DAD: I'm going to come with you guys and even if you do get the mouse I am going to take it from you and eat it. Eagle, go now and you bring the mouse to me.

EAGLE: OK. Imma do this for you because when I was little you helped me.

(EAGLE takes off.)

DAD: (Realizing TIGER is gone) Where did he go?

(DAD takes off for the tree.)

SCENE 2: At the tree

(TIGER arrives.)

TIGER: (To himself) I am already here.

(TIGER starts climbing the tree. Then, EAGLE comes and flies to the top of the tree, while TIGER is climbing it.)

(DAD arrives.)

DAD: I am faster than you.

(DAD catches up with TIGER, scratches TIGER in the back and TIGER falls off of the tree to the ground. TIGER scratches DAD in return. EAGLE grabs the MOUSE.)

EAGLE: I got the mouse.

(TIGER jumps up and bites EAGLE in the wing.)

EAGLE: Ouch!

(EAGLE and MOUSE fall down because EAGLE cannot control himself with only one working wing. TIGER and DAD have a showdown: TIGER scratches DAD in the face and DAD's eyes close.)

DAD: Ouch!

20

TIGER: *(Grabbing MOUSE)* I've got you.

(TIGER runs away with MOUSE.)

EAGLE: *(To DAD)* I'm sorry I let you down. I should have flown higher when I had the mouse.

DAD: You didn't let me down. He just jumps high. Let's forget about it. I'm just going to keep doing what I do and eat mice. Why doesn't my son just listen to me about eating mice instead of saving mice. I'm not worried about my son anymore because he disobeyed me about eating mice. *(DAD and EAGLE start to exit).* Just forget about him. Let's go home. My son will be fine by himself.

SCENE 3: Somewhere where nobody can find them.

MOUSE: Thank you for saving me back there. Why did you save me? Don't tigers eat mice?

TIGER: I do not eat mice. I think mice are innocent. You helped me find my way home when I was lost. Do you remember me?

MOUSE: Oh, you're that tiger! I am so happy to see you again.

TIGER: Now that I've saved you, I'm never going back home again. Me and you are going to have our own pride and all mice are welcome.

MOUSE: Thank you, can I bring my family?

TIGER: Yes, you can bring your family.

TIGER: *(To audience)* I've saved the mouse and now I am going to own my own pride and all mice are welcome. We are going to have a mouse and tiger party and all are welcome.

(MOUSE's family enters and they all party. Dancing.)

End of Play

The Bacon's Revenge

by Featured Playwright Rachel Masterson

Characters:
MASTER BACON
LEON
MOM
DAD
BROTHER
SISTER
BUTLER, an evil butler
TOWN CRIER, Bacontown town crier
BACONS, bacons of Bacontown (as many bacons for which the cast will allow)
OLD WIZARD BACON (shortened to OWB in the script)
SNOBBY BACON, a self-contented bacon who would rather watch movies than do ... anything else
OLD MASTER PIG, a stupid and proud pig
PIG SIDEKICK

SCENE:

(Screams of bacon being cooked from offstage. Ad lib things like: "Nooo, don't cook me!" and "I'm too young to die!" etc.)

(Enter MASTER BACON.)

MASTER BACON: I cannot believe it. People keep eating us. They won't leave us alone. It is good I have brains. I just managed to slip away—not like Leon my best friend! This is what happened to Leon...

(Begin reenactment.)

We were in our sleeping bags/bacon packet reading a magazine, which was very good. I heard the fridge door creak open and I saw the face of the big, dumb butler. I knew he was coming for us by the evil smile spread across his evil face.

(BUTLER opens fridge, in reenactment.)

I jumped out onto the cold floor. My bacon toes were freezing! I scurried to the little pouch on the side of the fridge for sauces. As I hid behind the soy sauce I saw the butler's big hand grab Leon. It was too late—he was just about to escape, to slip out, to be alive. *(Hand takes LEON.)* When I crept out to see if the butler had done any other damage *(Creeping out)* he was actually gone. I heard one last terrified scream from Leon before he was put on the stove to cook!

(End of reenactment.)

I am six weeks old, almost grown up. I am hiding in the pig shed where pigs don't eat me because I am made out of their friends' ears. I am 10 inches, very tall. I am slim with some fat. Everyone is getting eaten and I hate it. Yesterday *(Sobbing)* my brother got eaten by the dumb old butler. He said it tastes good. I want to try to eat his ear off for revenge. It just happens that I can't eat human ears as they eat pigs'. Today I am writing in the pig shed, the great place to be today. The pigs seem very sad. It must be because another pig got turned into a lot of bacon pieces, today. A bacon's life: born today, cooked tomorrow. Let me sneak away to see what the people are doing.

(Enter BROTHER and BUTLER. MASTER BACON sneaks to where the humans are and hides.)

BUTLER: I love bacon. We should have a bacon day.

BROTHER: Yes I love bacon, too. I wish we could eat all the bacon and could have some of it every day. What about in two days?

BUTLER: Or, we can eat all of them now! And we can throw the leftovers in the trash … if we have some… *(Evil laugh)*

BROTHER: Go fetch me some bacon, Butler.

(Exit BROTHER and BUTLER.)

MASTER BACON: How and why do people love bacon? I don't get it? Once my cousin tried to eat himself and he said he tasted horrible. So why do people keep on eating and loving us?

(MASTER BACON runs on little bacon legs to the kitchen.)

MASTER BACON: Bacon Town Crier! Bacon Town Crier!

(TOWN CRIER enters.)

TOWN CRIER: Yes, sir.

MASTER BACON: Tell all the bacons to come to the pantry at once!

TOWN CRIER: OK sir.

MASTER BACON: The town crier calls everyone, "Sir."

(TOWN CRIER goes to the refrigerator and opens the door.)

TOWN CRIER: *(Shouting)* Come to the pantry at once!

SNOBBY BACON: I'm in the middle of a movie. Why can't this just wait?

TOWN CRIER: Master Bacon is calling, sir. Sorry, sir.

(The BACONS leave the fridge and assemble at Bacon Town Hall. MASTER BACON sighs and checks his watch as they slowly assemble.)

TOWN CRIER: Hear ye! Hear ye! The people of the Bacon Empire...

MASTER BACON: Keep it short. We the Empire of Bacon are in danger. All of us are going to be eaten at dinner tonight and the rest of us are going to be thrown in the trash. The dumb old butler and the family are going to eat us all. *(Crowd gasps)* But, we're not doomed yet. We have to trick the humans—

SNOBBY BACON: What!! We can't trick the humans. They are smart and we don't even have a plan!

MASTER BACON: Okay, 1) I have a plan and 2) it will work. Come here Old Wizard Bacon.

(OWB stands up and walks to the front, in his hunchback way.)

OWB: *(In his crackly voice)* What do you want me to do?

MASTER BACON: I want you to turn yourself into a human kid and trick the brother and sister to come into the barn.

OWB: Yes, sir.

(OWB walks back to his place.)

MASTER BACON: *(Somewhere during this monologue, all of the BACONS except the OWB leave.)* Okay bacons, I only need you guys to do one thing. Hide. I'm going to get Old Wizard Bacon to talk to the kids and make them vegetarian. He is going to say to them, "Shame on you for eating bacon. Turn vegetarian or else." If you hide and do everything I say, my plan will work! After my plan works, think about what will happen to our humble Bacon Empire! Things will be different; really different! We won't have to live on the edge, not be scared every second of our lives. And we can have close friends over for breakfast knowing they won't be eaten. Close friends, like Leon. I know, I know, I was dumb to be very close friends with Leon but he was so nice, I couldn't just shoo him off. If my plan works, we won't have to fight about who has to sit closest to the door of the fridge, and we all know that the butler always reaches for the bacon closest to him. I could actually settle down. I could finally write that recipe book that I've always wanted to—*How To Cook: How to Make Everything Taste Good Without Bacon*. That's the life. *(Sigh)* I could actually rest. *(Smiles, deep in thought)* For years we have been hiding. We have been as scared as a fifth grader who is forced to eat asparagus! But now, once my plan works we will be as exhilarated as a teenager getting a new phone! *(Sigh)* I can't wait... Okay. Stop daydreaming, we have some work to do. We have to tell the pigs our plan because they are the best at making human voices and we need their help to make this plan work.

(Enter OLD MASTER PIG and PIG SIDEKICK from the shed.)

OLD MASTER PIG: *(Turning head around)* Hello, Master Bacon.

MASTER BACON: Old Master Pig, hello. How have you been doing?

OLD MASTER PIG: *(Shrugs)* Fine, just fine. *(Winks at other pig)*

MASTER BACON: *(Suspicious face)* Why did you wink?

OLD MASTER PIG: You caught me! We have heard about the "Butler Bacon Day" situation and we have made our own plan to stop him... Okay, okay, we will let you in on our most fabulous, daring, exhilarating *(Gasps from everyone)* plan!

MASTER BACON: We have a plan too. Tell us yours first. *(Raises eyebrows)*

OLD MASTER PIG: Well, we have decided to make them stop eating bacon.

MASTER BACON: *(Thoughtful face)* How are you going to do that...?

OLD MASTER PIG: Of course: after you guys get cooked I'll run into the kitchen and pour vegetable oil on you.

MASTER BACON: How do you know they don't like vegetable oil?

OLD MASTER PIG: What do you think? It has the word "vegetable" in it.

MASTER BACON: Okay. *(Thoughtfully)* Our plan is a little more complicated. So Old Wizard Bacon will turn into a human child and hide in the shed until we're ready. Old Wizard Bacon is going to convince the kids that bacon is bad and then the kids will convince their parents, as well.

OLD MASTER PIG: My plan rules. And your plan sucks. Am I right?

(PIG SIDEKICK cheers.)

OLD MASTER PIG: Oh, I have an idea. The person who wins gets to be master of the Pig Empire AND the Bacon Empire. And you bacon ... will be our slaves. *(Evil laugh)*

MASTER BACON: So be it. And when my plan works, everyone will have fair rights and everyone will stay alive and be nicer to each other.

(Groans from OWB. OWB falls to the ground, turning into a human kid about as big as the children.)

OLD WIZARD BACON: I look so young.

MASTER BACON: Old Wizard Bacon you look like a great child.

OWB: What should my name be?

MASTER BACON: Hmm *(Strokes chin)* let me see. Oh, I've got it: Bobby.

OWB: Sounds good.

MASTER BACON: Okay, get to work. No dillydallying.

OLD MASTER PIG: Come on pig, we have to practice being silent. I have to sneak into the kitchen and pour vegetable oil onto the bacon without being heard. Do you want your great leader getting caught? And even worse we will lose the bet and Master Bacon will rule you.

(Loudly, pigs practice tip-toeing into the kitchen, exiting.)

MASTER BACON: Okay, come on bacons. *(Enter SNOBBY BACON and one other bacon.)* In the kids' mother's voice, we are going to scream "come into the kitchen kids." That will make the kids come into the kitchen and Old Wizard Bacon will fulfill the rest of our plan. 1... 2... 3...

ALL OF THE BACON: *(As MOM)* Come into the kitchen, kids!

BROTHER and SISTER: *(From offstage)* Okay mom!

MASTER BACON: Yes we faked them out.

SNOBBY: They are so naïve. Stop being a bore.

(Sound of footsteps. All BACONS except OWB hide. Enter SISTER and BROTHER.)

SISTER: Mom, where are you? *(Looks for her, sees OLD WIZARD BACON.)* Who, are, you?

OWB: I'm Bobby, the new kid from across the street. I am here to make friends. Let's get something to eat. I am ravenous. *(Opens fridge)* Bacon, grrrrr-ross! *(Slams fridge door)* What is your problem? You know how fatty bacon is and bad for you, too?

SISTER: Eww! I want to be healthy.

MASTER BACON: *(Hidden, whispering)* Yes.

BROTHER: So what. I still love bacon no matter what you say.

OWB: You know that girl you have been crushing on since second grade? Well her dad had a heart attack because of bacon and if she sees your daily bacon at lunch, tsk tsk tsk, you will be toast. She won't even look at you.

BROTHER: For some reason I don't really like bacon any more.

OWB: Okay, I only need you to do one thing: convince your parents to not eat *bacon. (Shivers when he/she says "bacon.")*

(BROTHER and SISTER run off to parents' room. BACONS emerge.)

MASTER BACON: You were great!

OWB: Thanks, Master Bacon.

SNOBBY BACON: Ya right. *(Rolls eyes)*

(OWB glares at SNOBBY BACON. BROTHER and SISTER run back in and BACONS hide.)

SISTER: *(To OWB)* Easy peasy. I told Mom that bacon weakens your heart.

BROTHER: And I told Dad that bacon makes you worse at soccer. We all know how much Dad likes to win soccer games.

(All exit. OLD MASTER PIG and PIG SIDEKICK enter. In kitchen.)

OLD MASTER PIG: Come on pigs. Our plan is close to being in action. Okay so there are some bacons that are on the stove. The mother is already at the TV. What I need you to do is: go and scream to the family, "Honey! Kids! Our favorite movie is on." Then you run back. Remember to use the mother's voice. While they are at the TV, I will pour vegetable oil on the bacon. Ready, go!

(SIDEKICK PIG exits.)

SIDEKICK PIG: *(From offstage)* "Honey! Kids! Our favorite movie is on."

(OLD MASTER PIG scurries up onto the counter, gets vegetable oil and pours it on the cooked bacon.)

OLD MASTER PIG: Yes!

(OLD MASTER PIG scurries back to the pantry. DAD, BROTHER and BUTLER enter. They all eat bacon.)

DAD: Why is the bacon tasting so good today?

BROTHER: Yeah, it is delish.

BUTLER: I don't know. I was thinking it was rather tasty, too.

(DAD, BROTHER and BUTLER leave.)

OLD MASTER PIG: Rats.

(OLD MASTER PIG scurries off of the counter. MASTER BACON enters, looking bored, since he's been waiting around to see OLD MASTER PIG.)

MASTER BACON: My plan has worked perfectly. *(Eyebrows raised)* Yours...

OLD MASTER PIG: No it hasn't! The family is still eating bacon. In fact, they actually like it even better now because it has vegetable oil. *(Grin crosses face)*

MASTER BACON: Oh no! But, wait, your plan did not work either because they are still eating bacon and you made it worse because they like bacon even more now!

(Long pause. MASTER BACON's face frozen in mixed feelings expression. OWB runs in.)

OWB: I know. Master Bacon, your plan did work. I overheard the family saying that they would have one last try of eating bacon before they stop forever. *(Sigh of relief)*

OLD MASTER PIG: You win for now! Here you go: the Pig Empire Special Necklace. But, I will be back, to rule both of our kingdoms. Humph. *(Scurries away)*

(Enter all of the rest of the BACONS.)

ALL BACONS: Yay!

(Everyone goes to pantry.)

MASTER BACON: Bacon, and pigs, of our empire. I am here to say we have done it. We have made an impact on our small world. We won't need to live on the edge any more. We can relax! Go ahead, sleep in peace for once without being scared. Let me say it again: We have done it!

(All of the BACONS clap.)

End of Play

The Trip to the New World

by Featured Playwright Aijah T. Royal

Characters:

KATHREN, the main character. She is the one who wants to go to our human world.

SHANNYA, Kathren's friend from school. She wants to help Kathren but she does not want to go.

HANK, Kathren's father

PAUL, the one who is controlling Kathren and he won't let her go anywhere (some people say he is meaner than Kathren's father).

ROBBER

PERSON IN A SNOWMAN SUIT

SCENE 1: *In a hallway of a high school in a phone screen.*

(KATHREN enters.)

KATHREN: *(Rushing)* I got out of class and I need to tell Shannya something... I think Shannya's not gonna like me saying that I'm going to the real world. Here in High School World, we only get to walk around and go to school and that's it. Shannya likes it but I wish I I I I *(Breaking up with network difficulties)*. Uch! I need to remember to get the Wi-Fi password so I stop breaking up! This is so annoying! As I was saying to myself I wish I could go to the human world and see see see see *(More network difficulties)* how everything works out there. I bet the human world is more exciting than this High School Town. Also how am I going to get there? I know I can go go go go go find a a a a World Machine or I can jump out of the phone and replace my body with a dummy. Paul, he's the owner of the phone I am in, and doesn't want me to go to the real world since he doesn't like me! I'm so tired of people controlling me, especially Paul!

(SHANNYA enters.)

KATHREN: I have a plan to to to go to the human world. Would you like to come come come with me me me me? *(Network difficulties)*

SHANNYA: Uh, *(Thinking about what's going on)* sorry but if you want to do it today that will be great. No, I don't really want to go go go go. *(Network difficulties)*

KATHREN: Fine I'll just go on my own.

SHANNYA: OK well go have a blast without me.

KATHREN: OK!

SHANNYA: Oh my oh my. *(She sighs.)*

(SHANNYA exits.)

KATHREN: OK. *(She starts to call her dad. HANK enters as the phone rings.)* Hi Daddy um I need some money.

HANK: Why do you need money?

31

KATHREN: So I can buy a World Machine, because I want to go to the new world.

HANK: Are you crazy!!!

KATHREN: No. I just want to see the other side of the world for one week. *(She begs.)* Please Daddy please.

HANK: Oooo *(Breaking up)* OK but just for one week.

KATHREN: Thank you so much Daddy. *(KATHREN fills with excitement.)*

SCENE 2: *In the park.*

(KATHREN is looking at the World Machine, trying to figure out how it works.)

KATHREN: How does this thing work. I know! I just push this button and it will take me there.

(PAUL enters. He sees KATHREN and wonders what she is doing.)

PAUL: Where do you think you're going Kathren?

KATHREN: I'm going to your world so I can see what happens there.

PAUL: No I won't let you. You are lucky I made you a prep but if you leave I will make you a nerd when you come back.

KATHREN: No I won't because Xavier left and he is still a prep.

PAUL: That's only because I made him a prep again. I have the power to control this game.

KATHREN: I don't care what you say, I'm still going even if I turn into a nerd.

PAUL: Don't tell me I didn't warn you because I won't change you back if you leave.

KATHREN: That's fine with me. Now get me out of here.

(PAUL watches as KATHREN gets into the World Machine and starts it up.)

PAUL: Wait!

(PAUL hands KATHREN a slip of paper. KATHREN leaves in the World Machine.)

SCENE 3: *The New World.*

(KATHREN is looking around at The New World. She is in a park kind of like the one she was just in, except now she is in a big city. All around her are beautiful people and beautiful houses. It is very exciting.)

KATHREN: Wow this is so beautiful. Now what do I do? *(Suddenly a PERSON IN A SNOWMAN SUIT jumps out off the street at KATHREN!)* AH! What is that! I'm scared! I don't know what to do! I don't know anyone here! I think I should find Paul and I can ask him what to do.

(KATHREN walks around trying to find PAUL. It is getting hotter and hotter. KATHREN is becoming more scared. She does not recognize anything! A ROBBER enters in a ski mask.)

ROBBER: Give me your money!

KATHREN: What is this "money" you speak of and who are you?

ROBBER: I am a robber! Just give me all your money!

(KATHREN runs away, she is panicking.)

KATHREN: *(Yells)* Paul Paul! Where are you, Paul! Help me I don't know what to do.

(PAUL enters. He can see KATHREN but KATHREN can't see him, she can only hear him.)

PAUL: Do what you told me.

KATHREN: What did I say I wanted to do?

PAUL: You said, *(In a girl voice)* "I just want to see your world."

KATHREN: OK well I see it now. I am ready to go home.

PAUL: What do you mean you want to go home, you told your dad that you wanted to stay for a week.

KATHREN: I just want to go home. This is too much pressure, I realize I feel comfortable at home. Why are you always in my way?

PAUL: Because you need help!

KATHREN: I only need help when I ask and this is the only time I am asking! I need you to listen to me sometimes, because you are not always right!

PAUL: Of course I am not right all the time, but I am just trying to protect you, because you are in my game!

KATHREN: I like that you try to protect me, but I just really want to go home, but once I am there I need you to give me some more freedom. And of course then I will stay in your game!

PAUL: Fine fine. Where is the World Machine?

KATHREN: I don't know where it is. But the last time I saw it was in the park!

PAUL: OK but if your dad says something about you coming back early don't blame me.

KATHREN: I won't get in trouble I promise.

(All of the sudden KATHREN can see PAUL. They walk to the park and KATHREN gets into the World Machine and goes back home.)

HANK: Why are you back so early? You just left about 2 hours ago or was it *(Network difficulties)* it just now I don't know. I thought I had my vacation today!

KATHREN: But the good thing is I'm back h h h h *(Network difficulties)* home and I get to go back to school. And guess what!? *(KATHREN holds up the slip of paper.)* I've got the Wi-Fi password! It's "FREEDOM." I've missed being home!

End of Play

All the World's a Stage

by Featured Playwright Rose Duane

Characters:
XAVIER
LEVI
PROCRASTINATION
OLD WOMAN
COMPUTER

SCENE 1:

(XAVIER grabs the mail and shuffles to find the Great White Way Theater's letter.)

XAVIER: Today is the day! I got a letter from the Great White Way Theater, it's the theater I work for, and in this letter conceals the fate of whether or not my play will be produced! You see they approached me saying that they needed a new play to produce so I was chosen and *(XAVIER opens the letter.)* Ah! I'm writing a play! Think of it, something **I** wrote on stage in front of celebrities and filmmakers! I need to think of a play idea first... *(Xavier's smile lessens.)* I... I don't have any ideas. *(XAVIER feels sad and sits on the floor.)* Wh- what if I don't come up with an idea and my play is never produced... *(XAVIER lies on the ground, in existential crisis mode.)* MY LIFE IS OVER!!!!!!

(XAVIER's roommate LEVI walks in, pauses.)

LEVI: What are you doing?

XAVIER: My life is over, leave me to become one with the carpet.

(LEVI lies down next to XAVIER, face to face.)

LEVI: Why is your life over?

XAVIER: I won the chance to have my play produced.

(LEVI sits up.)

LEVI: Well that's not a life over situation, your life has only begun now.

XAVIER: Well, that's the problem! I have no ideas! I'm gonna be depressed, then I won't come to work, then I'll lose my job, then you'll kick me out, and soon I'm gonna be held up on the street asking, "Ma'am can you please spare some change?"

LEVI: You're being dramatic. All you need is some spaghetti, then I'll help you come up with an idea.

XAVIER: You will?

LEVI: Yeah, now come on I'm starving.

(Some time passes and they're done with their spaghetti dinner still with no play ideas.)

LEVI: Well I've got nothing.

XAVIER: Okay, well, it's been an hour, and I'm tired, so how about we go to bed, we'll go out tomorrow and search for play ideas.

LEVI: *(Yawns)* Okay.

(XAVIER yawns and goes to sleep. Stage lights dim and PROCRASTINATION enters and sits on a chair. Scene set to bedroom.)

PROCRASTINATION: Remember that 5th grade science project that you had to do? Make a board and explain how plants and trees grow. The teacher gave you 2 weeks to finish it, but you never got it done because I, Procrastination, was there to stop you. No one can see me. No, only me and other emotions can see me. But just like everyone else I've got your back, and I'm here to stop Xavier from starting that play.

SCENE 2: *Restaurant.*

(Lights turn brighter, it's the next day, scene set to restaurant. LEVI and XAVIER enter soon followed by PROCRASTINATION. PROCRASTINATION sits down.)

LEVI: Okay, so here we are in a crowded restaurant, surely you can figure out an idea by hearing a conversation or getting experience.

PROCRASTINATION: Yeah, right.

XAVIER: Okay, I'll go over here and you go over there.

LEVI: Got it.

(XAVIER goes left, LEVI goes right. PROCRASTINATION follows XAVIER.)

XAVIER: *(As he's walking he spots an OLD WOMAN and sits at a table next to her. PROCRASTINATION sits across from him.)* H- Hello.

OLD WOMAN: Well hello. *(Shakes hands)* You look a lot like my son.

XAVIER: Oh, really?

OLD WOMAN: He's quite dumb. Can never tell his right from left. Oh bless his heart though, he at least can stand to live on his own though. He has a great job, his job is as a bank teller and once he gave a person a 50 dollar bill instead of a 20 and said, "Keep the change." *(Continues to talk but PROCRASTINATION is starting to take control.)*

PROCRASTINATION: I think we need some cake. *(Finger gestures to the cake display)*

XAVIER: Excuse me ma'am, but I think I need some cake. *(Gets up and leaves.)*

SCENE 3: *Still in the restaurant.*

XAVIER: LEVI!

LEVI: Hey!

XAVIER: Did you find any stories?

LEVI: Well there was this one girl, Annabelle, and she was telling me all about how she caught her boyfriend Steven at the movies cheating on her with Julie, the most popular girl in school, and did you know tha-

XAVIER: Anything else?

LEVI: Well there was a single mother veteran raising two children.

XAVIER: Nothing good I'm going to the park, maybe there'll be no friend drama there.

SCENE 4: *Park.*

XAVIER: *(Sits on bench)* It's quite nice out very pretty, lots of people, lots of stories, now I just need to find an interesting event.

(XAVIER leans over, looking at the pond below him. As he sits watching he notices a reflection in the water as he looks up he sees a mother and daughter having a picnic. PROCRASTINATION notices.)

PROCRASTINATION: I don't think that's a story. *(Circles hand in air, signaling for the rain. Rain starts to pour. XAVIER leaves.)*

SCENE 5: *Xavier and Levi's apartment.*

(Rain is still pouring. Door closing sound, LEVI walks in finding XAVIER laying on the floor.)

LEVI: Find anything at the park?

XAVIER: I was watching some people for a while, but it started to rain.

LEVI: *(Looking out window)* It's still pouring out.

XAVIER: At this rate I'll never get an idea. Now my play won't be produced.

LEVI: *(Sits on chair)* Well how about we think about something here right now... Okay get this, how about your play is about a guy who runs a bar and in this bar he has silly yet life changing experiences, and there's a guy who walks in and every time he does everyone yells NORM!

XAVIER: That's *Cheers* and no.

LEVI: How about there's a teenage girl, and her mom forces her to move to her dad's house in a droopy dark place, and she meets this guy that she's head over heels for! But really he's a vampir-

XAVIER: *Twilight.*

LEVI: Okay, get this, 7 people go on a 3 hour boat tour an-

XAVIER: *Gilligan's Island,* no.

LEVI: Well, fine. If you're going to be grouchy about it then I just leave you to wallow in your own sorrow.

(LEVI exits.)

XAVIER: *(Speaking to audience)* I don't understand, why can't I, the guy who writes all the time, come up with anything? I mean here I am being mean to everyone just because I can't come up with anything. I'm frustrated, I really want to be a playwright, but I'm just scared if I do come up with an idea it won't be good enough. When I see a play or a movie the plot is amazing and the music is outstanding. I just want to be as good as the professionals.

(XAVIER exits, PROCRASTINATION enters.)

PROCRASTINATION: Wow I almost feel bad for him, if I could feel.

<u>SCENE 6:</u> *Xavier's bedroom.*

(Knocks on door, LEVI enters.)

LEVI: Hey, I brought you some pizza.

(XAVIER ignores him.)

LEVI: You know, it's not healthy to stay in bed all day. I know you're upset, but we can come up with an idea. An amazing idea that will blow any story out of this world.

(XAVIER still ignores him.)

LEVI: Do you want ice cream? A cannoli? *(Places pizza on night stand)* I can run out and get you something. *(XAVIER ignores him.)* Well, okay. Call me when you want something. I'll be at the theater. *(LEVI exits.)*

(XAVIER checks to see if he's gone, starts to eat the pizza, gets up and sits at the computer.)

XAVIER: *(Talking to the audience)* Okay, time to write. *(PROCRASTINATION pulls up chair and sits next to XAVIER.)*

XAVIER: Let's see title, title, title, title. Well, what's the story about? Let's search for ideas. *(Typing sounds)* Well it says that an idea can come from a life experience.

PROCRASTINATION: Hmph like your life was that interesting, very very boring you were born, you have a happy family and graduated college. Typical life.

XAVIER: Read a book, plagiarism, watch people and listen for ideas, ha! Like that works, brainstorming, oh ideas, ideas...

PROCRASTINATION: How about you watch a movie? *(PROCRASTINATION snaps finger at COMPUTER.)*

XAVIER: Oh! Netflix! What's popular now? No! I need to write this play. What if I wrote about this experience?! No, a person struggling to write is such a bad idea. Gosh! I'm such a bad writer, I don't write, I act!

PROCRASTINATION: Like your acting is any better. *(PROCRASTINATION waves at COMPUTER.)*

XAVIER: *(Confused)* Wha- What's with all of these pop-ups? *(There are clicking sounds.)*

(PROCRASTINATION gets up from chair and stands on top of the bed, next to a poster.)

PROCRASTINATION: *(Sighs)* I guess pop-ups aren't all that it takes. *(Rips off posters)*

(XAVIER walks to the bed.)

XAVIER: Gahh, the tape on these is terrible!

(When XAVIER moves back to the COMPUTER, PROCRASTINATION walks over to the bookshelf.)

PROCRASTINATION: This play will never be produced. *(Knocks books off of the shelf)*

(As XAVIER walks over to the books to pick them up PROCRASTINATION moves to the COMPUTER to put in a three hour update.)

COMPUTER: Update will begin in 3...

XAVIER: What?

COMPUTER: 2...

XAVIER: No!

COMPUTER: 1!

XAVIER: STOP!

COMPUTER: Update has begun!

XAVIER: Shoot. Since when did this start automatic updates?

PROCRASTINATION: Since I came into your life.

XAVIER: *(With hand gestures)* WHY DOES THIS HAPPEN TO ME? *(XAVIER walks back to bookshelf to continue picking up books. After looking at several books he notices his favorite.)* Oh, *The Westing Game*. A book about murder and money *(Chuckle)* but what if *(Grins)* there's a story about a girl ... who is invited to a party along with 8 people...

PROCRASTINATION: What?

XAVIER: They all know each other in real life but with the costumes they don't know who they are.

PROCRASTINATION: Stop thinking of ideas!

XAVIER: When everyone arrives at the house they receive a letter saying someone in the room is a murderer.

PROCRASTINATION: You *can't* write this play!

XAVIER: The main character's name is Taylor Edmin and when each guest disappears she goes searching for them...

PROCRASTINATION: I'm one sticker away from getting a water gun!

XAVIER: But when she is the last one left, she figures out they were dead the whole time.

PROCRASTINATION: Why would you do this to me? I thought we were friends!

(XAVIER scrambles for a pen and paper and starts to write.)

PROCRASTINATION: *(Shocked)* I- It was fun while it lasted but we'll see each other soon again. Very, very, soon.

(PROCRASTINATION exits.)

End of Play

The Ruler of All Worlds

by Featured Playwright Vanessa Iglesias

Characters:
JOE, a snowman
EMILY, the fairy
MR. RAINBOW

SCENE 1:

JOE: First. I am a snowman. My name is Joe. Everyone is scared of me because I am a snowman and I am living, and they think I am evil but I am not. I am happy and nice. I want to be the Ruler of All Worlds, But Emily the fairy will not let me. She is the secretary of the president Mr. Rainbow. She wants to rule the fairy world *and* the real worlds. I will get her. SHE IS EVIL I TELL YOU!

EMILY: Hi I am Emily the fairy. I want to be the Ruler of All Worlds to prove to my dad that I can do anything and that I am better than everyone even though when I was a kid he did not believe in me. But Joe the snowman wants to be the Ruler of All Worlds and he has a meeting with Mr. Rainbow the president in a week and three days to discuss his campaign.

SCENE 2:

(JOE walks in to MR. RAINBOW's office and EMILY is sitting at the front desk.)

EMILY: Hi how can I help you?

JOE: I came to see the president Mr. Rainbow.

EMILY: I am the secretary of Mr. Rainbow and he is busy right now. Sorry.

JOE: Do you know when I can talk to him?

EMILY: No. Sorry. Do you want to leave a message?

JOE: Tell him I want to be the Ruler of All Worlds because I think that I can make this world a better place to live in.

EMILY: Hhhey I want to be the Ruler of All Worlds because I think that I am the best person to lead the planets and so that I can prove my father wrong and show him that he is always wrong and I am always right.

JOE: That is too bad. I have a meeting with him today in 3 minutes.

EMILY: You are the guy that wants to beat me.

JOE: Uh ya.

EMILY: I will NOT tell Mr. Rainbow that you are here.

MR. RAINBOW: What were you not going to tell me?

EMILY: Nothing.

JOE: She means I am here. I am Joe the snowman and I have a meeting with you. *(JOE shakes MR. RAINBOW's hand.)*

MR. RAINBOW: Come in my office please. And Emily I will talk to you later.

(Both MR. RAINBOW and JOE walk into MR. RAINBOW's private office.)

JOE: Nice to finally meet you Mr. Rainbow! I could not stay still for the last 10 days, because I was just so excited to see you.

MR. RAINBOW: Thank you. What do you need?

JOE: I want to have an election to see if I can rule ALL the worlds.

MR. RAINBOW: No way because then you will take my role as president.

JOE: You can be president for the rest of your life if I am the ruler.

MR. RAINBOW: Well if you put it that way … yes.

JOE: But I want to have someone running against me please.

MR. RAINBOW: That's a first.

JOE: I want to win for who I am not because I am the only one running. If you let me have an election, I promise I will win.

MR. RAINBOW: Okay!

JOE: Thank you.

MR. RAINBOW: But who is going to run against you?

EMILY: I can go against him if you approve the election Mr. Rainbow.

JOE: Were you eavesdropping?

EMILY: Uh … ya.

JOE: You can go against me if you think you got what it takes.

EMILY: Seriously!? I got what it takes and more.

MR. RAINBOW: Are you sure about this you two?

JOE and EMILY: Ya.

MR. RAINBOW: You sure?!

JOE and EMILY: Yes.

EMILY: I am going to crush you.

JOE: I am going to crush you right back.

(EMILY and JOE are about to face off but then MR. RAINBOW stops them.)

MR. RAINBOW: Okay! The election is on May 24.

SCENE 3: *JOE and EMILY meet for lunch the day before the election. They are sitting at a table at a Chinese restaurant.*

(They sit down.)

EMILY: What are you doing to get all your votes?

JOE: I had my helper make t-shirts for the people who are going to vote for me. Also I made posters and books and pens, and I am going to put them all around the city so that people will know who I am and that I am running for Ruler of All Worlds.

EMILY: Well ... I made cupcakes.

JOE: What kind?

EMILY: Strawberry.

JOE: You do know that many people do not like strawberry and some are allergic to it.

EMILY: I know but the strawberry cupcakes were the cheapest.

JOE: Emily, Emily, Emily!

SCENE 4: *The day of the election.*

(Speaking to a crowd.)

JOE: Everyone vote for me, I have t-shirts and pens!

EMILY: Vote for me I have cupcakes!

JOE: If you vote for me all kids will have no homework. And parents, you will have ten breaks a day from your jobs so you can spend more time with your kids!

EMILY: If I win I will give out more cupcakes!

JOE: Time to see who won.

MR. RAINBOW: And the winner ... is JOE!

JOE: Oh my snowballs! I am so happy, thank you so much for voting for me!

EMILY: *(She doesn't really mean it)* Congratulations.

JOE: Emily, we will always be friends. *(Tries to shake EMILY's hand but she refuses.)*

EMILY: NO, I cannot be friends with someone who thinks they are better than me. And for all you guys ... no cupcakes. *(EMILY stuffs all the cupcakes in her mouth.)*

JOE: Okay.

SCENE 5:

JOE: I knew I would win ha! I am the best. And now no one is scared of me. You don't worry I will sign all your faces. I am so happy that you are all my friends now. I will miss you all. Now that I am the Ruler of All Worlds I am moving to space...

MR. RAINBOW: Space is not one of the worlds. I did not say you could rule space.

JOE: Oooooooo then I will move to Hawaii so that I can rule those Hawaiians and work there and swim all the time. Hasta la vista.

MR. RAINBOW: First you have to sign 1 bazillion forms for the people's health and education in the worlds.

JOE: What?? I should have read the forms before I signed up to be part of this election. Fine goodbye Hawaii.

EMILY: Haha hello Hawaii. That ticket can't go to waste. Where is it? So that I can go to swim with dolphins.

JOE: Why did I do this? Why?

End of Play

Ayo's Audience

by Featured Playwright Kaitlyn Murphy

Characters:
AYO
JAMES, Ayo's dad
MADISON, Ayo's friend
ROBERT
KAI
MARVIN, Robert's brother
DONNA

SCENE 1:

AYO: *(Confident, speaking loud)* I always dreamed that one day, I would perform a piece of spoken word written by me *(Points to self)* on stage. It would be so much fun, and all my friends would cheer. *(Points to self)* That I could change the way people think and view situations by only using words. *(Says timidly)* I'm actually really scared to go up on stage though. Forget going on stage, I can't even perform for my peers! But I'm working on it. *(Sighs then gets excited)* I guess today was my lucky day, because while walking to first period this morning I saw a flyer for a new after-school club. It starts tomorrow at 3:30 and it's all about artistic expression. They're looking for people who can dance, sing, draw, write—basically anyone interested in the performing arts. I've always loved to write. *(Starts to calm down)* I wonder how many students will show up. I'm sure it'll be fun. Besides, I've always said, "Live to inspire and to be inspired." *(While smiling)* I can't wait.

SCENE 2: Ayo's home.

(AYO is walking home from school in a rush. Walks through the door of her home. JAMES walks out of his room.)

JAMES: Where have you been? You're late.

(AYO scowls but still speaks respectfully.)

AYO: I rushed home as fast as I could. *(Checks watch)* It's only been 30 minutes since school let out.

JAMES: *(Grunts)* Mmhmm.

AYO: *(Looks up at JAMES)* My day was fine, how about yours?

JAMES: I had to clean up the mess you made this morning in the kitchen. Next time wash your dishes.

AYO: *(Mumbles)* I had a great day, Ayo. I'm sorry for not asking you how yours was.

JAMES: *(Rolls his eyes)* Stop being dramatic.

(AYO stays quiet for a while and tries changing the subject.)

AYO: I'm going to be a couple hours late from school tomorrow.

45

JAMES: Working tomorrow?

AYO: *(Hesitant about telling her father about the club)* No...

JAMES: So why are you going to be late?

AYO: ...There's this after-school club tomorrow it sounds fun ... and I really want to go.

JAMES: You don't have time for after-school clubs.

AYO: *(Getting a little frustrated)* Sure I do... It's only once a week.

JAMES: *(Grunts)* Mmhmm.

AYO: It's all about artistic expression... You know, the performing arts?

JAMES: Yeah yeah.

AYO: The flyer said we're going to have a drum circle and poets are going to perform.

(JAMES laughs.)

JAMES: So you're joining hippie camp?

(AYO becomes kind of offended.)

AYO: No... I just thought it might be fun.

JAMES: Whatever. Have fun in hippie camp.

(JAMES leaves the living room and enters his room.)

SCENE 3: *James's room.*

JAMES: When I was her age I wasn't worried about joining after-school clubs. I would go home, help out my parents. *(Shakes his head)* There's something wrong with that child. Always writing in that book of hers. Talking about how she wants to be a full time spoken word artist. What is that anyway? I bet it doesn't pay as much as a doctor, or a teacher. *(Sighs)* My youngest girl is going to grow up and be a starving artist. Well she better educate herself now because I won't be here forever. I expect her to become a respectable, independent young lady.

AYO: *(Still in the living room)* No matter what he says I'm going to have a great time.

SCENE 4: *School.*

(AYO is leaving class and heading to the first day of the club in a hurry.)

AYO: It's almost time to go. Class was sooo slow today. I feel like I've been here forever.

(MADISON gets up from her seat and approaches AYO in a friendly manner.)

46

MADISON: Hey, Ayo, what's up?

AYO: Nothing much. I'm going to the library.

MADISON: Girl don't you have anything better to do than study.

AYO: I'm not going to study. I've told you at least a million times that there's a new club starting today and I'm already late.

MADISON: Oh yeah that's right. I totally forgot. Well have fun. Me and Ty are going to the skate park. I got a new board and everything.

AYO: Have fun.

MADISON: See ya.

(AYO leaves the classroom after MADISON and runs downstairs to the school library. She gets to the library entrance and takes a deep breath. She can hear music inside the library. She is nervous and excited.)

AYO: It's gonna be fun.

(AYO walks into the library and sees a small group of people. She thinks she recognizes one boy in the group. He lives around her neighborhood but she's never talked to him. She stands next to him while people are mingling.)

ROBERT: Hey, welcome. My name is Rob.

AYO: Hey Rob.

(Shakes hand.)

AYO: I'm Ayo, nice to meet you. I think you live in my neighborhood.

ROBERT: Yeah I think I've seen you around.

KAI: *(Waves arms)* Let's gather.

(ROBERT smiles at AYO making her feel a little reassured. AYO walks over with the group and sits down. Everyone has a drum and starts playing a fast rhythm. ROBERT passes AYO a drum.)

ROBERT: Come on, just listen and then join in when you're ready.

AYO: *(Shaking her head)* I'm not really good at this type of thing.

ROBERT: Come on it's fun.

(AYO sits still for a moment listening to the sound of the drums and eventually starts playing with everyone. The beat gets faster after a while and slows down into an end.)

KAI: It's been about 10 minutes. Let's start the introductions. Who would like to start?

ROBERT: I'll start.

KAI: Okay.

ROBERT: Hey, my name is Rob. I'm 17 and in the 11th grade. Ummm... I guess I came today cuz I heard the drumming from my classroom and my brother told me about it. So yeah hey everyone.

KAI: Nice to meet you, Rob. Okay who's next?

DONNA: Hello, my name is Donna. I'm 15 and in the 9th grade. I'm here because I just felt good vibes here.

ALL: Hi, Donna.

AYO: Hey, I'm Ayo. I'm in the 9th grade, 15 years old. I like listening to music and writing. I joined because I thought it might be fun.

ALL: Hey, Ayo.

MARVIN: Hi! I'm Marvin, Robert's older brother. I'm 18 and am a senior. I've been in this program for 2 years now and it's awesome! I'm excited to be here this year. You guys are going to love it.

KAI: It's great to meet all of you. It seems like most of you guys have similar interests, so this will be fun. In the next two weeks, we're going to have a showcase of our work. I want everyone to make or prepare something for the showcase.

(Everyone starts talking about what they want to do for the showcase. AYO talks to ROBERT and the others and loses track of the time. She checks her phone to see the time.)

AYO: What time is it?

ROBERT: It's... 6:17.

AYO: OMG are you serious? I was supposed to be home by 5!

ROBERT: Yeah I should be getting home, too. Do you want me to walk you home?

AYO: I need to get home now so I think I'm gonna run. Thanks for the offer though. I got to go see you later.

(AYO tells everyone bye and rushes home as fast as possible. She finally gets outside of her home and runs inside. JAMES is sitting in the living room on his phone. AYO tries to be quiet and slip past him into her room.)

JAMES: Don't try to run past me. I see you.

(AYO sighs and walks back into the living room, knowing she's going to get a lecture.)

JAMES: Where have you been and why are you so late home? ...Not to mention you haven't been answering your phone.

AYO: Well I told you that I had a club after school today. And I kinda lost track of the time but we had soo much fun there was drumming and I met a couple new friends... I wasn't paying attention to my phone sorry.

JAMES: Sorry isn't going to cut it, Ayo... I knew I shouldn't have let you go. I let you have a little freedom but you can't even handle simple directions. Why should I let you go have fun when you can't even remember to do the things that you're supposed to do? I hope you had fun, because you're not going anymore.

AYO: I said I was sorry and it's not like you didn't know where I was.

JAMES: It's not up for discussion. You will go to school and come straight home afterwards. No park, no hanging out with friends and no stupid clubs.

(JAMES walks into his room and closes the door. AYO walks away quickly into her room and closes the door.)

AYO: He never listens to anything I say. I know I was kinda in the wrong but I told him I would be home late. It's not like I just got up and disappeared or anything... We were having so much fun... What am I going to do? He said I can't go back next week or stay after school anymore. This sucks... I even told everyone that I'd prepare something for the showcase... Sure, I was pretty nervous about it but this was my one chance to finally perform... I have to change his mind somehow... I'll work hard on it and then try to change his mind. I'll do whatever it takes to make him understand.

(Sits down and starts to write. Reads what she has.)

SCENE 5: *School.*

MADISON: Hey girl, what's up?

AYO: Nothing much.

(A moment of silence.)

MADISON: Soo what're you working on?

AYO: Remember that club I went to last week?

(MADISON nods her head.)

AYO: Well they're having this big showcase thing...

(MADISON interrupts.)

MADISON: Wait, hold up for a sec. Didn't your dad tell you that you couldn't go anymore?

AYO: Well yeah ... but listen.

MADISON: Oh gosh here we go.

AYO: Seriously, I've got a plan. I've decided to work hard. I'm gonna make a piece that everyone will love.

MADISON: Okay... Well what are you going to do about your...

(AYO interrupts.)

AYO: Well I figured I'd try asking him again... You know wait till he's calm first ... then I'm going to tell him everything ... let him know about spoken word and that participating in the arts is important to me.

MADISON: What if he doesn't listen?

AYO: He'll listen ... I hope.

(MADISON gets up.)

MADISON: Well if you're gonna convince him of anything, you'll need to get home on time.

AYO: Yeah.

(AYO puts her things into her backpack.)

AYO: Come on.

(MADISON and AYO walk downstairs and past the library, where they can see the club members talking. AYO stops for a second to look until MADISON grabs her arm.)

MADISON: Come on girl let's go.

(They leave the school.)

SCENE 6: *Ayo's home.*

(After talking with MADISON at school, AYO gets home before her older brother. AYO looks at her watch as she enters the house.)

AYO: Yes!! I got here first... Well, he definitely can't say I was late.

(JAMES enters the room.)

JAMES: You're here early. I thought you might be your brother.

AYO: No, it's me... So how was your day?

JAMES: Fine.

AYO: That's good... So I kinda wanted to talk about something with you.

(JAMES interrupts.)

JAMES: What were you doing up so late last night? I heard you from my room. What was that?

(AYO pauses.)

AYO: Did you like it?

JAMES: What is it? And I wasn't really listening but from what I heard, it sounded decent.

AYO: Well that's what I wanted to talk to you about... I didn't know you could hear me ... but I was reciting that thing I told you about a while ago ... spoken word?

JAMES: Oh so that's what it was.

AYO: Yeah I've been working on some and I would love it if you could listen to it sometime.

JAMES: You wrote it?

AYO: Yeah want to see some?

(JAMES hesitates for a moment.)

JAMES: Sure go ahead and show me.

(AYO rushes to her bag and pulls out her book. She opens the book and shows JAMES the pages filled with writing.)

AYO: This is what spoken word is... I've been writing it for a while but I've never performed any before.

(JAMES is silent.)

AYO: Ummm well I think I told you before but remember that club from a couple of weeks ago? ...They're having a showcase and I was supposed to get a chance to perform.

JAMES: I remember.

AYO: Well I've been working really hard on this and ... I promise to clean my messes and I'll call you if I'm ever gonna be late coming home again... Can I please perform, Dad? A chance like this may never happen again.

(JAMES is silent for a moment.)

JAMES: Are you really serious about this?

AYO: Yes... This is what I love doing.

(JAMES is silent for a while.)

JAMES: You're going to call me as soon as you leave school. You understand?

AYO: Yes.

JAMES: Also ... tell me the time and place of this performance.

(AYO becomes excited and extremely happy.)

AYO: You're coming?

JAMES: I don't see why not.

(AYO hugs her dad and continues to work on her poem right away.)

<u>SCENE 7</u>: Backstage at the performance.

(Backstage, everything is busy. AYO is pacing until ROBERT approaches her.)

ROBERT: Hey are you okay?

(AYO doesn't respond.)

ROBERT: Ayo... Ayo!

AYO: I'm sorry did you say something?

ROBERT: Yeah are you okay? What's with all the pacing?

AYO: Oh sorry I didn't even notice.

(AYO looks out into the audience.)

AYO: How... How many people are supposed to be here?

ROBERT: I'm not sure ... it could be up to a couple hundred.

AYO: A couple hundred!!!

(A moment of silence.)

ROBERT: Hey... By any chance... Are you afraid of the crowd?

AYO: Not afraid ... more like terrified.

(AYO looks out into the audience again.)

AYO: I don't even see my dad.

(A moment of silence.)

ROBERT: Hey it's not that bad... We're all going to be here to support you and I'm sure your dad's just a little late ... probably traffic or something.

AYO: Yeah you're right I'm sure that's all it is.

52

(ROBERT and AYO leave the stage and KAI comes out.)

KAI: Hello everyone! I'm Kai, one of the facilitators of Young Voices, and welcome to our showcase of 2015! Today, you will see performances by the students we work with here in Washington, DC. We hope you enjoy the show!

SCENE 8:

(JAMES comes in and sees AYO perform.)

AYO:
"Why I Write"
I write poetry because it's what I've always dreamed of
The words are spoken
The spoken words
Each and every thing I've ever heard
Everything I see or seen is why I write poetry
Before I could walk or talk they called me Black China Doll
And before I started writing I started identifying the words that touched or bruised
Any of the words that I used became fused to my memory
So now I put pencil to paper so you can see
What I can do or be with words that are heard
That can elate or disturb
That can inspire or if left to lay grow tired
And expire or even stagnate
I write as a weapon of mass destruction against inhumanity
I would rather write than die
Having never expressed or shared a word in prose
Having come so close to succeeding
There by leading a revolution against ignorant thinking
And as we fight that good fight
It's all the reasons I write
I'll write if you be my muse
If you stand up and refuse to be silent and instead be vigilant
While speaking your peace
Because at the very least it is something
And something is always better than nothing
I am a writer and I have a story to tell
You can ask anyone who knows me and they'll tell you
I'll tell you that story in detail
I am me
I'm all that you see
But not all that I can be

End of Play

Mrs. Chang

by Featured Playwright Nanichi Vargas

Characters:
MRS. CHANG
LING, her daughter
NEWSPAPER MAN
MYSTERIOUS MAN/DR. HIXELSTINE
WILL CHANG

SCENE 1:

MRS. CHANG: *(Struggling to the stage with a cane. She speaks with an old woman's voice.)* Oh! Well hello there, I... I... I... I can't see you, come closer, well then that's more like it. Okay my name is Mrs. Chang. I am the wife of Mr. Chang who is sadly no longer with us. Oh he ... he was such a fine man nice and handsome, well anyway, it's been so long since he died and my daughter, Ling, does not trust I can still take care of myself, so she wants to put me in an old folk's home. My daughter has grown to be a smart and beautiful woman but she's wrong about putting me in an old folk's home. Besides, all the people are well ... old! Well yes I know I'm old, but not that old plus everyone knows Mrs. Chang can still boogie! Well maybe I shouldn't say that, my grandchild said it wasn't cool. Well whatever it was in my day ha, ha, ha! Oh... I miss those days, and I'd do anything to go back.

(LING walks onstage with grocery bags in each hand.)

LING: Nín hǎo. *(She breathes heavily, carrying the bags as if they are extremely heavy.)* I brought you some food Mom, I got off work early, so I thought I would come home to make sure you're not dead.

MRS. CHANG: *(Cuts her eyes at her daughter and speaks with a mean voice)* Oh! How lovely, you're so kind.

LING: Listen Mother... You... You know I love you right, and I'm just looking out for you... I just can't trust you living alone.

(LING puts the bags on the floor, and slowly walks to her mother with open arms.)

MRS. CHANG: *(Gives her daughter a mean look and turns away)* I can handle myself... Oh and thanks for the food but you can go now I'm going to take a nap ... alone ... in my bed ... in my house ... all alone, now leave and go take care of my grandchildren. Why don't you teach them how to respect their mother so that later in life they won't annoy you as much as you annoy me. *(Turns to the audience)* Man that felt good, this old lady is on fire.

LING: *(Gasps)* Wow Mom, okay well damn... I mean I'm just trying to look out for you. I'll leave if you want me to.

(LING turns around and walks offstage.)

(MRS. CHANG walks towards a bed on stage right and climbs inside. She turns towards the audience.)

MRS. CHANG: What the hell y'all lookin at ... you see something cute, oh wait it's me of course. I know I know you think I was a little too harsh on her right... I know I think so too, but you can't redo the past, as much as I would like to ... just to see my beloved Will again. Soooo! Y'all gonna leave or are you going to watch me sleep? Well since y'all not moving I'm going to consider all of you as some creeps and I'm going to sleep anyway.

(MRS. CHANG lies down and a bright green light shines on her.)

SCENE 2: The setting is in the daytime, the stage has been transformed into New York's Chinatown in the 1960s, there are buildings, people (mainly Chinese) and children run with firecrackers and rockets. In walks a young beautiful woman.

NEWSPAPER MAN: Newspapers! Come and get your newspapers.

(MRS. CHANG walks to the NEWSPAPER MAN.)

NEWSPAPER MAN: Well hello young lady come buy the new edition newspaper of 1965.

MRS. CHANG: What, why did you call me a young lady, and it's not 1965!

NEWSPAPER MAN: I'm sorry, you must be some kind of crazy person because it is 1965.

MRS. CHANG: What this is impossible. But I'm kind of liking this.

(MRS. CHANG walks around and is followed by a MYSTERIOUS MAN.)

MYSTERIOUS MAN: Mad is what they call me, but mad I am not. My name is Dr. Hixelstine and I believe in the ability to travel through time. Once I saw ... um ... um, Mrs. Chang? Yes that's her name, I knew she had come from the future, but I just need to find out how.

(MRS. CHANG walks into a diner and DR. HIXELSTINE follows her inside.)

DR. HIXELSTINE: Stop! Mrs. Chang you're coming with me.

MRS. CHANG: What, but I didn't do anything, I mean I am just a simple and all ordinary young girl. Man it feels nice to say that.

DR. HIXELSTINE: What why do you say that?

MRS. CHANG: Um... Um... Uh... Uh... Well I don't know.

DR. HIXELSTINE: Okay, and people call me mad. Well anyway you're still coming with me.

(He grabs MRS. CHANG by the hand and pulls her all the way to his lab.)

DR. HIXELSTINE: Will! Go get the antidote.

(DR. HIXELSTINE does an evil laugh.)

MRS. CHANG: Will? I know that name it belonged to my husband, Will Chang, and it's funny because I still remember meeting him at a laboratory such as this one! Oh my lord ... it's ... it's ... it's you! It's been so long... I miss you and love you deeply.

(MRS. CHANG reaches towards WILL. There is a long pause.)

WILL: What are you talking about it's me, well of course, the only question is who are you, lovely lady?

(WILL holds MRS. CHANG by the waist.)

MRS. CHANG: *(Lets herself free from his arms)* I'm Elizabeth, my name is Elizabeth.

(MRS. CHANG looks into a mirror on the wall, and sees that she is not herself when she was young.)

MRS. CHANG: What who am I! Who is this person I am pretending to be?

WILL: What are you talking about, you are Elizabeth aren't you?

MRS. CHANG: *(Turns and faces the audience)* What to do, what to say. I can't tell him my real name which is Elizabeth by the way. I need to make up a person to pretend to be for the time being, and he will meet the real me later on. *(Turns and faces WILL)* No! I am not Elizabeth, you're so funny, my real name is um ... um ... um ... um ... Mary.

WILL: Well then Mary, um ... shall we go?

MRS. CHANG: *(Turns and faces the audience)* What go where? Oh! I have a strong feeling I shouldn't do this, he needs to meet the real me and fall in love with the real me, man I miss my life, my daughter, my grandchildren. I have to confess to Dr. Hixelstine even if, it means getting, killed by his poisoned antidote.

WILL: Mary, I... I have to tell you. Dr. Hixelstine is evil! He pulled me away from my family, which was very poor, making me think life would be better for me, but no, now I'm his slave.

MRS. CHANG: Will ... I ... I must confess. I am from the future. Dr. Hixelstine suspects me and, I'm sorry but my time has come to go. But please hear me out, there will be a beautiful girl ... her name will be Elizabeth and you two will soon fall in love, trust me please!

(MRS. CHANG walks to exit the stage and DR. HIXELSTINE cuts in front of her.)

DR. HIXELSTINE: Will! Bring me the antidote.

(WILL gives DR. HIXELSTINE a giant needle.)

DR. HIXELSTINE: Now! ...And her name is most definitely not Mary!

WILL: Why do you say that, she just told me her name was Mary?

DR. HIXELSTINE: Well it isn't... Her name is Sofia.

(DR. HIXELSTINE puts the antidote on the floor.)

DR. HIXELSTINE: She was and forever will be my one true love ... and she should be dead!

MRS. CHANG: *(Begins to shout)* What the hell is this!

DR. HIXELSTINE: *(Shouts back at MRS. CHANG)* I am not mad, I am not mad, I am not mad, I am not mad... *(He stops shouting.)* You're supposed to be dead... Mrs. Chang how selfish can you be? What of Sofia's family, you can't make them forget about their only child.

MRS. CHANG: I don't understand. Who is Sofia? ...Why must I be dead?

DR. HIXELSTINE: When you go back in time you're not yourself ... instead you're a dead corpse brought back to life to protect your true identity...

(He turns to WILL and begins to shout again.)

DR. HIXELSTINE: Get out ... out I said!

(WILL exits the stage.)

MRS. CHANG: If you're not mad then why did you enslave my future husband ever since he was a young boy! ...And how are you the only one who knows about time travel?

DR. HIXELSTINE: I was born a very rare breed of human... A breed that no longer exists, but somehow survived within me. I have this strange ability to see the future, and there were others like me but they died in the ancient world. Will was about five years old when I got this vision of you traveling back in time to meet Will, the love of your life, again. So that is why I enslaved him and I waited for your arrival. Time travel is not something you can just create with technology and computers ... but it's something I brought with me when I was mistakenly unharmed during the Earth's renaissance.

MRS. CHANG: Are... Are ... you immortal?

DR. HIXELSTINE: Yes... But I cannot choose who I am, I did not ask for it ... to be immortal ... I don't want it... But we can't redo our mistakes, this is why you are not yourself, instead you are someone else who has finished their time on Earth. But ... this person you pretend to be had a life, they had a family, love, pain, a home ... and if you steal their identity the memory of that person and all the people who loved that person are lost... I am not mad, I made it my purpose to make things right with selfish people like you.

MRS. CHANG: How am I selfish... You take a young boy away from his family on your behalf ... and you say I am selfish just so I can see my beloved again, how dare you!

DR.HIXELSITNE: You really don't understand now do you! I am the good guy. *(He picks up the antidote.)* This antidote is ancient medicine deadly to regular humans, but not to those who travel through time... Do you know why you're here? Because you felt so desperately that you needed to see your beloved again! But did you know that bringing my Sofia back to life not only makes her family forget her but makes every single family on Earth forget a loved one. How does that make you feel? I am here to help, Mrs. Chang, I've seen the future, you and Will live a glorious life together, don't risk the life of every single person on Earth so you can live your perfect life again!

MRS. CHANG: I ... understand.

(MRS. CHANG lays down on the floor, as DR. HIXELSTINE motions to stick her with the needle, a green light shines, then the curtains close.)

SCENE 3: *The curtains open, on stage lays the bed from the first scene, and the grocery bags on the floor.*

MRS. CHANG: What! I'm... I'm home again and I'm old again!

(MRS. CHANG turns and faces the audience.)

MRS. CHANG: Wow! Going back in time was amazing. But I think... Well... I love my life now, I love my daughter and her children. I'm happy right here, right now.

LING: *(She walks on stage)* Listen I should have listened to you before ... and I'm sorry if you want to live on your own, it's your life and my ... I mean your decision.

MRS. CHANG: No! ...You were right I've raised you well, because you really care about me and I don't want to be alone, but I also don't want to be alone with a bunch of strangers either.

LING: I understand, please come live with me and my kids, this way I won't have to go to bed every night worried I may not see you the next morning.

(LING walks towards her mother and they hug.)

End of Play

Like Father, Like Son

by Featured Playwright Dominique Butler

Characters:
DOMINIQUE (DOMO)
A.P.
JUNEBUG
MOM
DAD
POLICE OFFICER 1
POLICE OFFICER 2
OFFICER JOSH
ANT
Feel free to double cast where necessary

NEIGHBORHOOD:
4700 Simple City SE, Washington, DC

SCENE 1:

(It is a hot summer day on the streets of DC. DOMINIQUE is standing at the corner of Benning Road and Alabama Avenue. The block is filled with police. DOMINIQUE's DAD is going to jail. His DAD is usually not around anyway, but for some reason DOMINIQUE looks up to him. DOMINIQUE's DAD doesn't know how much his jail time affects him.)

A.P.: Domo, look your pops going in again.

DOMO: I know I think he ain't going to ever come home.

A.P.: Yea my mother told me my pops been in since I was five.

DOMO: I'm starting to think this nigga don't love me.

A.P.: I be thinking the same thing but it be making me mad.

JUNEBUG: Wassup y'all why you look like that?

DOMO and A.P.: Look like what, fool?

JUNEBUG: Y'all look somebody dead or something.

DOMO: No ain't nobody dead but my pops went in.

JUNEBUG: What he do doe?

DOMO: I really don't know but when we were coming from my pops' house he told me go by the Ave and wait for him. I was waiting for like fifteen minutes and then he pull up in a Camaro and told me get in. I got in, we went to the gas station and the feds were there. It seem like they didn't notice us but as soon as we pulled off they was on our ass. My pops was speeding and finally lost them. That's when we pull up on the Ave and he told me he was about to go. I said, "Where?" He said, "Far away," and then ran in the house and before he could go the peoples pull up and took him and there was a truancy van riding past. And then A.P. walked up.

(JUNEBUG pats his back.)

JUNEBUG: Damn, bro, I hope you be okay.

DOMO: I don't know this time. Bro, I'm getting tired of this shit.

A.P.: Don't do nuffin dumb like last time, pimp. You know how when you get mad you like to take cars and shit.

DOMO: I don't know how to cope with this. Last time he was home he told me he ain't going back and it seemed so true. Then three months later he's going back.

A.P.: Yea that's wild but you know why he be outside doing the shit he doing, right?

DOMO: Yeah I know but he coulda got a job.

A.P.: He could but a job ain't going to keep them J's on your feet, pimp.

DOMO: I'm hip but growing up with no pops is worse than having Payless shoes on, kill.

A.P.: A look doe! I don't want you to sit around and be mad all day. Let's go out with the gang tonight.

DOMO: Kool where we going doe?

A.P.: Somewhere with all the females cuz you know the females love the gang pimp. But my sister having a party doe.

DOMO: Duhh we from Simp, it's our lifestyle. But thanks, pimp, for making me feel better.

A.P.: Ain't nuffin, pimp. That's why we men. But go get dressed. I'mma come knock on the door inna hour.

DOMO: Already.

SCENE 2: *Domo's apartment.*

(DOMO's apartment building is in the projects. It is small and packed and the doors are close to each other and the hallway lights don't work. The halls are dirty with tobacco wrappers and condoms. DOMO goes in the apartment. The apartment is dim and crowded with objects.)

MOM: *(As she walks in his room)* Dominique, your dad called you.

DOMO: When did he call?

MOM: About thirty minutes ago. He said he was calling back in a couple of minutes.

DOMO: Okay.

(The phone rings as he sits down. DOMO answers the phone. SOUND CUE: "You have a collect call from Jessup Correctional Facility.")

DAD: Hello.

DOMO: Hello ... Dad.

DAD: Yea, I'm sorry. I know you mad and wanna know why.

DOMO: Nah I don't care about you. All you care about is yourself.

DAD: That's not true. I love you, boy.

DOMO: Then why you keep getting locked up? What you say last time you came home?

DAD: I said I wasn't getting locked up again... But...

DOMO: Ard and what you do? I'm tired of it. Why you keep lying to me, Dad?!!?

DAD: I'm trying but it's hard.

(SOUND CUE: "You have five minutes left.")

DOMO: I know but my mother wants to talk to you. See you soon.

(Gives the phone to MOM. DOMO leaves the room.)

MOM: You got my son talking crazy, Ty!

DAD: I ain't got him doing nuffin. He is his own person.

MOM: And what type of person are you? *(As she hangs up)* Boy, come here. *(DOMO comes back in.)* You are talking like you lost your mind.

DOMO: You don't understand! Nobody understands! How much I need him. Who goin' to teach me how to be a man, Ma?

MOM: Well I always said I can't teach you how to be a man, but I never said I couldn't help you, baby. When are you going to realize that you are in charge of your life? You let your father control your life. It's his way or no way.

DOMO: I just feel he understand me better.

MOM: Who be here all your life?

DOMO: You.

63

MOM: Who always tell you you're smart, handsome and strong?

DOMO: You.

MOM: You are the key to my heart. Baby, you don't need him. I got you.

(DOMO flashes a fake smile.)

DOMO: I know, Mom. You right.

(MOM gives him a hug and rubs on his back.)

MOM: I love you, boy.

DOMO: I love you too.

SCENE 3:

(It is about 8 o'clock. DOMO is getting dressed. He puts on his black pants with all the zippers and a black hoodie. Lastly, he puts on his Timbs. Then there is a knock on the door.)

DOMO: Who is it?

A.P.: It's A.P., bro.

DOMO: Oh. *(Unlocks the door)* I was just putting on my Timbs.

A.P.: Damn everybody got they Timbs on. We bouta look sweet. But I can tell you not feeling good you got on all black bro.

DOMO: I'm good, pimp. I look sweet doe.

A.P.: Yea you do doe.

DOMO: But come on we gone … hold on let me get some money. Ay Ma can I get like $30?

MA: I don't have it, Dominique!

DOMO: Ardd Ma I'm gone. *(Slams the door)*

(They are walking out the building.)

A.P.: Why you doing your mother like that, bro?

DOMO: Because fool every time I ask her for some cash she say she don't have it but my pops always give me money.

A.P.: Here bro. *(Goes in his pockets and gives him $30)* I'm only giving you this because I see anger in your eyes.

DOMO: Thanks fool.

A.P.: Ain't nuffin. I hope my sister didn't bring no wild ass girls to her party because if she did I'mma be sick.

DOMO: Kill, but I was going to step. Anyway I was going to get some gas.

A.P.: You still smoke fool? I been stopped. I be too high sometimes.

DOMO: Times like this I gotta blow.

A.P.: Yea okay.

JUNEBUG: Y'all ready?

A.P.: *(Hard look on his face)* We all ready pimp.

DOMO: Hold up. Let me go get a car, bro.

A.P.: What!? A car? You tripping. Why you want to get a car, Domo?

DOMO: Because I'm not in the mood for a bus.

A.P.: Well I'm not fuckin with it. It's way too hot out here and you wanna steal a car.

DOMO: Man you always think you know something. Ain't nobody worried bout us, pimp. Just come on.

A.P.: Nah, pimp I ain't bouta do that. I'mma hop on the bus.

DOMO: So you going to let me take the car by myself? What type of friend is you, pimp?

A.P.: I'm the type of friend that will tell you when something is not right and try to stop you from doing it. But you are your own person.

DOMO: Yeah ard, pimp, go ahead. I know wassup now.

A.P.: Whatever, pimp. You ain't you right now. Ayy J.B., watch him. I'm gone.

JUNEBUG: Ardd pimp.

DOMO: So what now? You ain't coming now?

JUNEBUG: Man you know I'm rocking with you, pimp.

DOMO: Ard we gone uptop.

JUNEBUG: What kind of car we getting?

DOMO: Nuffin too new because that would be too noticeable.

JUNEBUG: Damn I want this Jeep at least then.

DOMO: Ard hold up let me see if I can get it. *(Touches the doors)* It's already unlocked pimp. We gone.

JUNEBUG: Hold on, pimp. *(Looks around)* I gotta funny feeling about this.

DOMO: Aw man come on, pimp. We good.

JUNEBUG: Ard pimp.

DOMO: Sit down here in the driver's seat while I go under the hood real quick.

JUNEBUG: And hurry up doe.

DOMO: Ard pimp ease up. *(DOMO is under the hood for about seven minutes.)* Hit the gas pedal, pimp.

JUNEBUG: Ard. *(Taps the gas pedal. Alarm goes off in the car.)* What the fuck is that Domo?

DOMO: Come on J.B. here come the peoples.

(DOMO starts to run offstage. Two POLICE OFFICERS enter from both directions. One grabs JUNEBUG. The other chases DOMO. JUNEBUG jumps out of the car and falls.)

JUNEBUG: Domo help!

POLICE OFFICER 1: Ay stay down. Don't move. Put your hands behind your back.

JUNEBUG: Okay okay!!

(POLICE OFFICER 1 handcuffs JUNEBUG. DOMO is running. As he looks back and sees JUNEBUG on the ground, he stops. All the actors freeze except DOMO. POLICE OFFICER 2 is chasing him and is close enough to grab him.)

DOMO: What do I do? I never been locked up. I promised my mother that I wouldn't get in no trouble. I know she's going to be upset. What would my pops do? Probably leave his friend. I hate to be like him. I won't be like him. I'm my own man.

(The actors unfreeze.)

POLICE OFFICER 2: Freeze! Don't move. Put your hands over your head and keep quiet.

(POLICE OFFICER 2 grabs DOMO. Both POLICE OFFICERS read JUNEBUG and DOMO their Miranda rights.)

SCENE 4: A week later.

(There are 250 kids in this jail in orange jumpsuits. There are 5 units, 10 people per unit and 2 guards per unit. There are 5 rooms in the units, 4 people per room.)

OFFICER JOSH: What's your last name again?

DOMO: *(Stands up)* Butler. Why?

OFFICER JOSH: Is your father's name Ty?

DOMO: Yea how you know?

OFFICER JOSH: When I was working over at the adults' jail there was a Butler.

DOMO: Oh.

OFFICER JOSH: Yeah. *(Reaches in his mailbag)* You have this letter from your dad too.

DOMO: Thanks.

(DOME waits until OFFICER JOSH walks out of the cell to read it. DAD comes out and reads the letter out loud on the other side of the stage while DOMO looks at the letter.)

DAD:

> Dear Dominique,
>
> How you doing baby boy? Hope you didn't think you getting locked up was going to make me come home any faster. I'm still here. You should feel real dumb right now, baby boy. You getting locked up didn't hurt nobody but yourself. It has an effect on people but life goes on. Your mother loves you and so do I, but we can't make you do nuffin you don't wanna do cause you gotta see for yourself. These streets ain't no joke slim. You think every time somebody make you mad you can just lunch out? And nothing's gonna happen to you? You keep that up, you'll be over here with me in the big boy jail, not that playground. I never knew that my actions had a big effect on you. But then again I knew and I'm sorry. Forgive me. I can't live with knowing my son hates me. Write me back.
>
> Your Pops.
>
> P.S. Did you meet Officer Josh yet?

SCENE 5:

(DOMO comes home after 3 months.)

A.P.: Damn pimp you been home for a week now. How ya feelin?

DOMO: I feel better and wiser but when the last you seen Junebug?

A.P.: Yea he come home a week before you did.

DOMO: Let's knock on his door.

A.P.: His mother sent him to live with his grandmother out in Philly.

DOMO: That's probably for the better.

A.P.: Why you say that?

DOMO: Because it's nothing but trouble around here. It's like we stuck with no right. Just all wrong.

A.P.: Damn jail really did change you.

DOMO: Yea it has. And I want to tell you thank you for trying to stop me from taking that car. I'm glad to have you as a brother.

A.P.: Ain't nuffin pimp. A1 day 1 shit.

(ANT walks up.)

ANT: Wassup pimp! I ain't seen you in a minute. When you get out?

DOMO: A week ago.

ANT: Kill ain't nuffin. Hang with me. I still got it. *(Pulls out some keys)* Let's spend the block one time pimp.

DOMO: What! Fuck nah fool. I'm not doing shit. See A.P., how can I do right with all wrong around me? I'm goin in the house.

A.P.: *(Smiles)* Ard pimp.

SCENE 6:

(DOMO walks up into the apartment building and goes in the house.)

MOM: Dominique, come here baby.

DOMO: Okay. *(Walks to her room)* Yes?

MOM: Did you see your friends?

DOMO: Yes.

MOM: What they say?

DOMO: Nuffin. They were glad to see I was home and they said I changed a lot.

MOM: You have and I'm so glad you did.

DOMO: Me too.

MOM: Did you ever write your father back?

DOMO: No I wasn't ready to but now I am.

MOM: Here. *(Hands him pen and paper)*

(DOMO goes in his room and starts writing.)

DOMO:

Dear Pops,

Sorry I took so long to write you back. I wasn't really understanding what you was asking me but I'm home now and I'm a changed person. You could change too if you put your mind to it. The only reason I got locked up was just to see why you were coming in and out. I see now that that life ain't for me. I know who Officer Josh is too. He the one that gave me your letter. I wanna know when you coming home and are you going to be changed like me? And oh yea Pops I'm using my head now. I told Ant I don't mess with him because he asked me to drive a stolen car! My mind is way stronger now, Pops. And everything you said was right and I do forgive you, Dad. When you come home I hope you ready to be a changed man because I need you!

Your son,
Dominique

P.S. Call me when you could.

End of Play

Sophia and Ernesto

by Featured Playwright Dania Canales

Characters:
SOPHIA, Ernesto's sister
ERNESTO, Sophia's brother
OFFICER
JUDGE

SCENE 1: *Sophia's living room, late at night, after the accident.*

(SOPHIA talks to the audience.)

SOPHIA: People might judge me for what I did. But, believe me I have a reason for what I have done. I didn't commit any crime, it was dark at night, my brother wasn't on his five senses. He was scared, he was in shock! He couldn't believe what he did. I told him to run away. It was too breaking for me to see him in this situation. I would never confess the truth, I will never say what really happened that night. No matter what I will try to protect my brother. I know this is against my religion, but my brother can't go to prison, because it is all my fault for not stopping him. Even if he doesn't care about me and my feelings I still want to protect him from going to jail, I know we both grew up in very different environments but we still part of each other, and I know he loves me deeply, inside his heart he cares.

(SOPHIA bends over and starts praying silently.)

SCENE 2: *Sophia's living room, 12 hours earlier, that morning.*

(ERNESTO comes in and looks at SOPHIA, gives her funny looks and laughs at her.)

ERNESTO: My sister is always worried about me, oh my gosh! That is so freaking annoying, she worries for no reason. I know what I'm doing and that is only my business not hers. She is nobody to control my life. I do what I want, I party, drink and go out with my friends. "Come on" that's what I love to do; I haven't lived with her all my life since my parents brought her here from Panama. My life has completely changed. She takes life too serious. She is a freaking chent.

(ERNESTO notices SOPHIA.)

ERNESTO: Hahaha! There she is again … hahaha! What a chent!

(SOPHIA keeps praying.)

SCENE 3: *Sophia and Ernesto's school.*

(SOPHIA enters.)

SOPHIA: Science class is almost over and my brother didn't show up today. I wonder where he might be, I need to call him but I can't right now. I'll wait until the bell rings.

71

(Bell ringing... Dang, dang, dang... SOPHIA gets out her cell phone and calls her brother. Ring, ring, ring, ring. ERNESTO enters.)

ERNESTO: Oh my God! My sister again... *(ERNESTO answers the phone.)* What the heck do you want?

SOPHIA: Where are you at? What's all the noises in the background? Are you out of school? Please tell me you are not at your friend's house!

ERNESTO: Que te importa? Not your business! And yes I am at my friend's house doing what I love to do, just leave me alone ma'am! Damn! Bye.

(ERNESTO hangs up the phone call.)

<u>SCENE 4:</u>

(SOPHIA gets home from school. Her parents are not at home yet; they are working. When she gets home she is hoping to find her brother at home but to her surprise he is not there either.)

SOPHIA: What if I call him again? But I know he is not gonna answer my call; I have a better idea! I'll go find him.

(SOPHIA arrives at ERNESTO's friend's house and knocks the door. ERNESTO opens the door all drunk and smoking a cigarette.)

ERNESTO: Oh hey sister come on in have a beer with us! Come and enjoy our party, let's have fun together... Here drink this beer.

SOPHIA: What are you doing, you know I don't drink! I came here to take you with me, please let's go home. It's almost 10pm and our parents are going to get home and they will notice that we are not at home. Let's go, I brought Mom's car!

ERNESTO: Give me that! *(ERNESTO takes the car's key.)* I will drive. I am on my five senses, I am not drunk at all. *(ERNESTO is almost falling off drunk while saying this.)*

SOPHIA: Give me my keys back, of course I won't let you drive. You are all drunk—almost falling. I will drive... Give it to me please, give it to me! I'm asking you politely, let's go. Leave that beer there and let's go.

(ERNESTO leaves the beer and gets out of the house with the car keys. SOPHIA runs after him. ERNESTO is already in the car, the car is on and he is ready to drive. SOPHIA gets in the car.)

ERNESTO: Sophia hurry up! Let's go home before our parents get there.

SOPHIA: Of course we are not going anywhere please let me drive.

(ERNESTO starts driving and speeding up.)

ERNESTO: Wooohooo!!!! I love to speed!!! Oh yes, oh yes!!!!

SOPHIA: Ernesto please slow down we are gonna have an accident!! Please slow down, and let me drive.

(Suddenly they see a woman crossing the street. ERNESTO tries to slow down but he is speeding too fast, so that when he stops it is too late and he has run over the lady. All he hears is SOPHIA screaming.)

ERNESTO: Oh my God tell me I am just having a horrible nightmare, tell me it's not true what I'm thinking just happened...

(They both get out of the car, ERNESTO kneels down screaming and crying and kind of in shock at the same time ... suddenly there is a deep silence between SOPHIA and her brother.)

SOPHIA: Ernesto run away, run awaaaay!!! It's not your fault run away.

ERNESTO: No it's not your fault, you are innocent it's all my fault and I can't leave you here in this problem. Call the police.

(SOPHIA pushes ERNESTO.)

SOPHIA: Run away, run away Ernesto! Go home before our parents get there!

(ERNESTO finally runs... SOPHIA hears a police siren arriving to the scene, the OFFICER gets out of the car.)

OFFICER: Good evening ma'am... License please. *(SOPHIA gives him her license.)* Were you the one who was driving?

SOPHIA: Yes sir.

OFFICER: You know you are in a very serious situation right? ...Do you know she is dead?

SOPHIA: *(Nervously)* ...Yes sir...

OFFICER: Do you know you can be charged with so many things ... and the very first one is you killing this woman and the second is you driving at ten without somebody else who has a license. You can't be driving right now you are not 18 years old. You will have to stay here with us until your parents arrive. We have to ask you a couple more questions.

SCENE 5:

(Several weeks have gone by, and SOPHIA and her family are getting ready to go to the court hearing. Her brother ERNESTO has been deeply depressed and his parents are wondering why? ...He doesn't even want to go to school he is crying all the time.)

ERNESTO: *(Dramatically crying)* Oh my god I can't take this anymore. My conscience is driving me crazy. I must confess the truth!! Sophia does not deserve to be in trouble just because of my immature and stupid actions. It's me who has to be in her position right now, she is innocent, you know what? Imma confess everything today during the trial.

(SOPHIA, ERNESTO and their family arrive in court ... they are ready to begin the trial.)

JUDGE: Good morning everyone, as you all know we are here because Sophia has been accused of killing Marie Mayer, this incident took place on Henderson Street at 10:07pm and we all know this is a very serious situation.

(Suddenly at the back of the room ERNESTO gets up and nervously starts talking.)

ERNESTO: First of all, I'm really sorry to interrupt you sir, but I can't take this anymore, this is killing me. *(ERNESTO starts crying.)* Sophia didn't kill Mrs. Mayer, she wasn't driving, I was drunk and I didn't let her drive. She told me to run away because she didn't want me to get in trouble.

(SOPHIA gets up.)

SOPHIA: Ernesto please stop! Stop don't say anything.

ERNESTO: No Sophia, we both know you have been lying to protect me.

(SOPHIA starts crying, ERNESTO runs towards her and hugs her.)

ERNESTO: I love you Sophia, can you forgive me?

SOPHIA: *(Looks at her brother)* You forgive *me*, because I promised you not to say anything but I failed.

JUDGE: *(Speaking in a mad voice)* Enough... Sophia, why have you been lying to us? Do you even know that it is a very serious deal? Hiding someone is a serious situation, you have violated the law and you will face penalties now for two major crimes, hiding important information, and driving underage. Ernesto if this is found to be true, you are going to face charges as well.

(SOPHIA runs towards her brother and hugs him.)

SOPHIA: *(To her brother, both crying)* Don't worry baby everything is going to be okay. Just be faithful and pray to God and He will give you strength.

ERNESTO: Now is when I realize that I was wrong and you were always right when you used to give me advice. I love you so much! Now you are in this because of me, please forgive me!

JUDGE: We will have to proceed with this investigation and we are going to have another trial to determine what is going to happen with both of you, everybody is dismissed.

SOPHIA: Ernesto we don't know what is coming for us, but I want you to stay strong until the end, and regardless to what might happen never forget that I love you so much and I want you to come to church with me and accept Christ in your heart as your one and only savior.

ERNESTO: Yes!! We are going straight to church I'm going to listen to you this time. I don't want to ruin my life anymore.

End of Play

The New World

by Featured Playwright James Domchick

Characters:
PROFESSOR IAGO
KELLAN (Young Iago)
DANNY MILLER
DAD
NATHAIR

SCENE 1:

(It is the year 2015 underground, in an abandoned bomb shelter with hexagonal walls. The walls are covered in machinery, monitors and cameras recording his progress in his experiments. He is wearing a worn out black lab coat with torn ends. He has long hair, which is in disarray, but is clean-shaven. His name is PROFESSOR KELLAN IAGO.)

(Looking out into the audience, open to interpretation.)

PROFESSOR IAGO: I have not been out of my lab for months for fear I would be found and forced to stop my experiments. I have been working on the next step of human evolution. I wish I was allowed to work freely but there are many who call me "mad," "crazy," "demented," "insane," the "herald of the end" and even the "Devil." For science I have persevered working diligently, never wavering in my conviction. Humanity has become a lifeless husk that should be discarded like a wrapper on a piece of candy that you especially want. To jumpstart humanity into a new age a great change is needed. This great change shall be the birth of my children who will usher in an age of modified homo sapiens. The world has become stale and I am the only one who can stir it along with my children.

SCENE 2:

(Flash back to a younger version of KELLAN IAGO at age 15 in a bright lab dissecting a crocodile. He is wearing a black lab coat and muttering to himself.)

KELLAN: They think of me as they would a tottering five year old but they do not know the extent of my genius. The world has yet to recognize me for what I am, a true genius. Einstein, Currie, Watson and Crick and Darwin combined could not reach my level of ascension. I have ascended so far that I do not consider myself human. I have never considered myself as human, when I was younger I often thought I was some kind of alien. I was smarter than the other kids, and I knew it. My teachers hated me because I did not disdain to do their work at home. I always finished it in class, and I had no friends as no one could hold my magnificent intellect. Therefore I spent most of my childhood looking out at the world as a separate entity, an entity that scorned me, shunned me and exiled me into a world of loneliness that only my two-headed snake was able to pull me out of.

(DANNY MILLER walks in, he is a middle-aged man. He is wearing a standard white lab coat that seems to light up in the bright room. He has a British accent.)

DANNY: Oi Kellan, are you almost done with that croc? We are about to leave for the night.

KELLAN: Go ahead and leave then, I am not done yet.

DANNY: I can't leave you here alone! It's against lab policy to leave a child alone in a lab.

KELLAN: I am no child, in most nations I would be considered an adult.

DANNY: Well in this country you are, so get out of here.

KELLAN: Just because I am a child in body does not mean I am a child in mind.

DANNY: Fine, stay here but good luck explaining it to the boss.

(DANNY leaves muttering something about how KELLAN is a know-it-all brat and he should have never crossed the pond.)

KELLAN: They supervise me without recognizing my great intellect, just because of the length of my life. If humans are such an enlightened race, then why do they judge me by my age and not my intellect?

(With a shake of his head KELLAN puts the crocodile in the freezer to preserve it, then walks out still wearing his black lab coat. As he walks away he takes one last look at the lab before leaving.)

SCENE 3: At KELLAN's house, a rundown one-floor house with the light on in the living room on the left.

(After leaving the lab, KELLAN appears to be hesitant to go inside. Using his key to open the door he walks past the couch where his DAD is drunk and sleeping. His DAD is in his thirties and is a mechanic. He has resented KELLAN for his brilliance. His mother was killed in an "accident" but KELLAN knows it was his father and despises him for it. KELLAN goes to his room on the first floor, a room with no windows and only one door, a room originally meant for a storage space. His walls are covered in ideas he has had and drawings he made related to his ideas. While walking up to his favorite drawing, a drawing of a humanoid snake...)

KELLAN: You would understand me Nathair, you would not judge me by my age or looks but by my intellect. I swear that one day you and your brothers and sisters will usher in a new era in history that will redefine the term "human." But what to call my creations as a whole... The Unnamed. That is perfect, a name is only as good as the creature anyway and it is not overly specific.

(He takes one last look at the drawing before lying down to read his genealogy book.)

SCENE 4: Flash-forward back to the current time where PROFESSOR IAGO is standing near a humanoid-sized tube awaiting the finishing of the education that he created using rapid imagery projected into the back of his eyes.

PROFESSOR IAGO: I can barely contain myself, after all this time the first one is ready to leave the pod. After working at that atrocious college which tossed me out for "corrupting" the students and using college resources to help me finish my research on animal and human genealogy ... they said that they could not handle my obsession any more, but like all other humans they were afraid of the extent of my intellect. They got what was coming to them when I took their equipment for myself.

(A humanoid snake-like creature emerges from the pod somewhat dazed.)

NATHAIR: (In a naturally intimidating voice) Hello Father, when will my sistersss and brothersss be done?

PROFESSOR IAGO: Soon, then we will no longer need to hide from the world, and they will be forced to reconsider what makes one human and how they treat others.

NATHAIR: That ssseems a worthy goal Father, but why do they ssscorn and hate you?

PROFESSOR IAGO: Because they fear what they do not know, backed by those who wish for human superiority on this Earth.

NATHAIR: Then why are you alone? Sssurely there are thosse who agree with your views.

PROFESSOR IAGO: Yes but none of them are able to keep up with my intellect or can be trusted. You see my enemies are very devious in their underhanded tactics to get me to stop my experiments, but after all these years you are finally "born."

NATHAIR: I was human once before you modified my geniusss right?

PROFESSOR IAGO: *(Dismissively)* Yes, I assume you want to know who your parents were?

NATHAIR: Yesss, I would like to know Father.

PROFESSOR IAGO: *(Dismissively as if it is not worth the time it takes to say the words. Sighs)* Okay, I had wished to save this until later after you got to go outside the lab but now is as good a time as any. You were an orphan abandoned to foster services when you were still a baby, the humans who were your parents did not want you because you had twelve toes, instead of the traditional ten. This deformity was common in Egyptian royalty so I took you from that terrible orphanage.

NATHAIR: Then I would like to thank you Father for sssaving my life, and honoring me with being your general.

PROFESSOR IAGO: I know, now come we must make haste to another lab. The military will be here soon.

End of Play

A Nobody!

by Featured Playwright Edward Wade

Characters:
MOM
TIM
SARAH
RANDY
BUS DRIVER
MS. EVENS
BONNIE
MAX
JANET
DAD
DAVE
MS. HARPER

ACT I, SCENE 1: _Tim's house._

(The bright sun rises as my alarm goes off every morning. Each morning before school, I wake up at 7:30am or else I would never be able get up and get dressed and make it to school on time.)

MOM: Rise and shine Tim, you'll be late for school. I'll get breakfast ready while you prepare for school, you don't want to be late for your first class so hurry.

TIM: _(Gaspppp)_ I'm up, I'm up.

MOM: Breakfast's ready Tim, would you like burnt toast or crispy toast? Your pick!

TIM: Mom I'm not in the mood for breakfast today.

MOM: Are you sure? It's bad to go to school on an empty stomach, don't you think? Wait is something wrong? You look kind of down.

TIM: Nothing I'm all right, it's just sometimes people always picking on me especially Randy, he always make fun of me because of my butt chin.

MOM: You know if anything is going on at school, you can let me or your dad know. Do you need me to find out where he lives and have a talk with his mom?

TIM: Mom it's fine I'll be good. _(Beep, beep)_ There is the school bus. Love you Mom.

BUS DRIVER: Hey kid.

RANDY: Look everyone it's butt face. _(Everyone laughs.)_

SARAH: Are you done?

79

RANDY: Yeah.

SARAH: Good then let's talk about what we're doing Friday night instead of messing around with this nobody.

RANDY: *(Gassp)* Aww really, already? I was just getting started.

BUS DRIVER: Now, now, everyone calm down, have a seat, and leave poor Tim alone. All he wants is to be somebody, and you all treat him like trash.

ACT I, SCENE 2: *School first period.*

(The first bell rings and first period begins. The teacher is out and the class will have a substitute for her absences, which is an elderly lady MS. EVENS who's in her seventies.)

MS. EVENS: Good morning boys and girls, I'm Ms. Evens. I'll be your substitute teacher for the week and will be filling in for Ms. Harper because of her private excuses. Any questions?

(Silence.)

MS. EVENS: Well let's start with today's lesson, OK! Now, which of you would like to read today's objective?

(SARAH raises her hand.)

SARAH: Me.

MS. EVENS: All right go for it.

SARAH: By the end of today all students will certainly be able to analyze and cite evidence on the story *Bullies Always Learn*. Students will read pages 40-55 using Brief Response with at least 5-8 sentences.

MS. EVENS: Thanks uh, uh uh—

SARAH: Sarah.

MS. EVENS: Right Sarah, OK class now Sarah has read the objective and we know what our goal is by the end of class, now pull out the book your teacher had you reading the other day and read.

BONNNIE: But Ms. Harper reads to the class! We actually read together then do today's lesson.

MS.EVENS: Well we can read together, no problem! Would you like to read the first page?

BONNIE: No thanks.

MS. EVENS: Would anyone like to read?

(Silence.)

MS. EVENS: Well I'll just call on someone, uhh you right there! *(She points.)* Will you read for us?

RANDY: Sure...

(Door opens and a new student walks in.)

MS. EVENS: How may I help you, do you have a pass?

MAX: I'm a new student here, today is my first day.

MS. EVENS: Well hello, and what's your name?

MAX: Max Yung.

MS. EVENS: Well you can start your day off by having a seat by this young gentleman in the back, what's your name sweetheart?

TIM: Timothy Brown.

MS. EVENS: Alright Mr. Brown, may you remove your books off the desk next to you?

(TIM trips and falls and everyone laughs.)

RANDY: What a loser.

MS. EVENS: Now that's no way to talk to our peers, apologize then begin reading the first page please and thank you!

RANDY: Sorry! *(Whispers)* Loser.

MAX: *(Whispers)* I didn't find that funny they just jerks.

TIM: *(Whispers)* It's cool 3 years of this takes some getting used to.

MAX: I'm Max by the way.

TIM: I'm Tim.

(Shaking hands.)

ACT I, SCENE 3: *Girls' locker room.*

(The girls are just getting out of gym class and entering the locker room as usual.)

BONNIE: Sarah you're going to that party with us Friday right?

SARAH: Sorry girls, I promised Randy I'd go with him and he promised me and after we're going to get pizza and heading to his house for ice cream.

JANET: Girl ever since you've been talking to Randy you've had no time for us at all.

SARAH: Well Saturday I'm free let's hit the mall, I got to get a few outfits anyways.

BONNIE: That kid Tim had me DTFL in class earlier today.

JANET: Yeah... Wassup with that kid anyways?

SARAH: I don't know, I know his dad is the priest of my grandmother's church... Wait... Speaking of that would you guys please go with me to church on Sunday, my grandmother is forcing me to go and I don't want to be bored there.

BONNIE: Really, but the last time we were there over 4 hours and I nearly fell asleep and that's rude and embarrassing.

JANET: I can't sit in one spot for too long, uh um, not me.

SARAH: Well then, let me text Randy and let him know I'm free Saturday and want to hit the mall.

BONNIE: All right, fine...

JANET: Girl you know I was going to go anyways.

SARAH: Right...

ACT II, SCENE 1: Tim riding in the car with his dad.

(School lets out and right before TIM is ready to step on the bus to leave his DAD beeps the horn to get his attention.)

DAD: Hey Tim, I was in the area and thought I'd come get you from school since I'm near anyways.

TIM: Wassup Dad, you know you didn't have to come get me, I know how you hate wasting gas so much sometimes because of how expensive the gas is.

DAD: That's OK son, you know, sometimes is not all the times. There are times when God tells you to do something and you do it.

TIM: So there's a reason He was telling you to come get me.

DAD: Must be, just know sometimes God gives you a sign and He gives you signs for a reason and when you reveal them signs you follow them and you'll see where it gets you.

ACT II, SCENE 2: On the bus ride home.

(Everyone on the bus is having separate conversation and waiting on their stop.)

RANDY: That kid Tim lucky his dad came to pick him up today, I was going to embarrass him in front of everyone on the bus just to get a laugh by throwing water in his lap to seem as if he piss himself. But don't worry I'm going to run into him again soon.

DAVE: (Laughing) Little bastard, you'll get him Randy.

SARAH: I know this isn't none of my business but just to correct you, he's actually not a bastard his parents are happily married and both in his life.

82

RANDY: How do you know?

SARAH: Because... His father's a priest his mom is a part of the choir and he's an usher, they're all members of my grandmother's church.

DAVE: He still a bastard.

MAX: And you're a jerk.

DAVE: Who are you talking to tough guy!

MAX: You!

RANDY: Is there a problem?

SARAH: Guys don't.

RANDY: Mind your business Sarah this has nothing to do with you.

SARAH: This is my business when there's bullying involved, you know Randy you're starting to act exactly like the character from the book *Bullies Always Learn*. You're a real jerk you know that right.

DAVE: Whose side are you on?

SARAH: Max's obviously.

RANDY: Well he's about to get dealt with.

SARAH: That doesn't make sense, and besides you touch him and we're done.

RANDY: Let him live.

Dave: What... Never.

RANDY: Just let him go dude! If you ever come across us again just know we're going to have a problem.

MAX: Right, right problems, OK!

ACT II, SCENE 3: *In the house on Facebook.*

(TIM is on Facebook and gets a new friend request from MAX, the new student. They start having a conversation.)

MAX: Hey Tim.

TIM: Yeah.

MAX: I have something to tell you about that kid Randy.

TIM: Me and Randy are not on good terms, anything you have to say about him I could care less about.

MAX: It actually involves you.

TIM: Really what is it?

MAX: Well earlier today on the bus he was saying that he was going to embarrass you if your dad hadn't came to get you after school, and Dave kinda said some words, then I said something then they were about to jump me and Sarah kinda defended me.

TIM: What a jerk I wish someone would do something about those guys.

MAX: I was thinking the same but I figured it should be you and I, because he'd done something disrespectful to us both and I'm not having it.

TIM: Randy would get the whole football team and get us jumped then have us even more embarrassed and disrespected.

MAX: Someone got to do it, hey but I overheard these two girls talking and there's a party right down the street from my house, you want to go?

TIM: And where is this?

MAX: On W Street down by the white church there.

TIM: Wait I know exactly where that is, I'm actually a member of that church.

MAX: Great I'll try to stop by this Sunday but is that a yes?

TIM: I'm not sure.

MAX: Why not it'll be fun, just go.

TIM: I'm sure it'll be fun but I don't know how my parents will react to that.

MAX: There will be plenty of girls there.

TIM: Alright, I'll go but let's just go to your house right after school Friday then go to the party from there.

ACT III, SCENE 1: First period.

(Friday morning the bell rings, first period begins and the teacher is back.)

MS. HARPER: Hey everyone I'm so sorry I've been out for the last few days, I had family issues and private problems, so! Let's get our day started all right... Young man I'm not sure this is your class, are you trespassing?

MAX: I'm a new student I started this Wednesday when the sub Ms. Evens was here.

MS. HARPER: Well I'm Ms. Harper and may I see your schedule?

MAX: I lost it.

MS. HARPER: I'm afraid I will have to get a dean over here to be sure.

TIM: No Ms. Harper he's not lying he's a new student, just started two days ago.

MS. HARPER: But I have to report this or I may lose my job so—

TIM: Wait I have proof, the sub left a note on the desk saying that she already been through all this yesterday.

MS. HARPER: Well then, welcome! Mr. Brown I can see you finally made a friend.

TIM: Yeah.

MS. HARPER: By the way, where is everyone? I know it's Friday but I didn't know it was skip day.

TIM and MAX: I don't know.

ACT III, SCENE 2: Max's house.

(Friday evening MAX and TIM are in MAX's house going to the party.)

TIM: This party is going to be something big.

MAX: I know right, I could just feel it, something really bad is going to happen.

TIM: You see now I'm having second thoughts about going.

MAX: Come on I was just kidding, everything is going to be just fine.

TIM: All right let's go.

MAX: Let's go then.

ACT III, SCENE 3: At the party.

(Party is crowded, everyone dancing and having fun, and TIM bumps into SARAH and greets her with a hello. She ignores him but he keeps trying get her attention, and she decides to talk to him to get to know him better, and TIM starts talking about RANDY, then they start a conversation and get rudely interrupted by RANDY.)

RANDY: Why are you here? Why are you talking to my girl?

SARAH: We were just talking about how bad you've been treating him and Max, and I was thinking we've all been treating him very badly and don't like it.

RANDY: Whose side are you on? So you choosing sides?

MAX: Why don't you just go away and leave us alone!

RANDY: Didn't I tell you not to come across me again?

TIM: Dude just leave!

DAVE: Awww look who decided to finally stand up for his-self.

RANDY: You sure you want this tuff guy?

SARAH: Randy, STOP!

DAVE: Let's show them who the tuff guys are.

(RANDY punches TIM then MAX punches DAVE. This starts a big fight and the party is stopped.)

SARAH: You guys stop.

DAVE: Everyone run the police are here.

RANDY: We gone come on Sarah.

SARAH: No I'm not going, we're done Randy!

RANDY: Fine!

SARAH: Fine, just GO! We're done! Oh my gosh I am so sorry, are you guys all right?

MAX: I'm fine, Tim seems to need help.

SARAH: Are you OK? Look I'm so sorry for however I ever treated you before, but just know after today I think you're really brave and I thought wrong about you, and I would like to apologize.

TIM: I'm fine, I'm OK, we're good.

SARAH: Good, look, don't worry about him he's a jerk he always seem to have a high temper.

TIM: It's nothing, really.

MAX: Come let's head to my house to heal you up and get you ice.

SARAH: I'll help, I know you can't carry him alone, besides I don't have anything else to do.

(As SARAH walks with TIM and MAX she begins to get to know them better and decides to stay and help out with TIM and watch movies and eat popcorn and as she's sitting with them she starts to fall for TIM.)

ACT III, SCENE 4: The mall.

(TIM and MAX decide to go to the mall to get MAX a suit for church and run they into SARAH and her friends.)

TIM: Hey there's Sarah, hey Sarah!

SARAH: Oh hey what are you guys doing here?

MAX: We're getting me an outfit for church tomorrow.

SARAH: Oh you guys going to church tomorrow, we're going too.

BONNIE: Excuse us for one second. *(Pulls SARAH over by JANET)* Why are you conversing with them?

SARAH: Don't worry they cool, they are actually cooler than what we thought.

JANET: Tim and Max are you blind, are you coming down with a cold or something?

SARAH: No, look they're cool how 'bout I prove it. Let's go to eat pizza with them while we're here, it'll be fun.

BONNIE: You sure about this?

SARAH: Positive.

BONNIE and JANET: OK.

SARAH: Tim, Max, this is Bonnie and Janet, my two best friends.

TIM: Hey I'm Tim this here is Max we're friends of Sarah.

BONNIE: Yeah, we know.

SARAH: Wow, it's weird we both decided to come to the mall today, last night was fun we should go hang out the five of us.

MAX: Sure why not?

TIM: It's fine to me, where we going to go first?

BONNIE: We can stop for ice cream.

JANET: No! We should stop for pizza.

SARAH: Oww, how about both?

TIM: I'm in!

MAX: Me too, whatever Tim with I'm with.

(The day is going well and everyone is enjoying themselves and having a good time. They meet up at church the next day since they're all going. At church everyone is listening to the choir sing and praising the Lord and dancing, enjoying their time together and becoming good and close friends. And so TIM, MAX, SARAH, BONNIE and JANET become a fivesome, they all are close friends and are together almost every day, and TIM and SARAH eventually start dating.)

End of Play

Finalists

Untitled

by Finalist Natan Bokretzion

Characters:
KING WEREWOLF
WITCH
KING VAMPIRE
KING ZOMBIE
SOLDIER

SCENE:

KING WEREWOLF: What a happy day! The whole palace is peaceful, everything is happy—

(WITCH appears out of nowhere.)

WITCH: I will curse you, King Werewolf! You have to get the diamond from the Altamore Cave and eat it before midnight. If you don't, the whole world will die. And the only person who can go is you, King Werewolf!

(The WITCH vanishes. KING ZOMBIE and KING VAMPIRE are peeking and hear the prophecy.)

KING VAMPIRE: Yes! If we stop King Werewolf from getting the diamond we can get our revenge and be the rulers!

KING ZOMBIE: Yeah, many many years ago, before I died and before you were bitten by a vampire—

KING VAMPIRE: Yeah that really hurt!

KING ZOMBIE: Stop interrupting me, idiot! Where was I? Oh yes. Many many years ago, when the werewolves invited the vampires and zombies to a party, when we were just dancing and drinking wine, a zombie and a vampire got drunk and accidentally killed a werewolf! That's when the King Werewolf banished us for life. But now we will get our revenge!

(KING VAMPIRE and KING ZOMBIE sneak off.)

KING WEREWOLF: Should I ... get that witch back and kill her ... or should I go? I have an idea—I should go. But I have one question—where's Altamore Cave?

SOLDIER: I told you sir, you should have studied.

KING WEREWOLF: Don't interrupt me! I've been studying in my dreams and I'm going to cut your neck out for saying that. And by the way, where is it again?

SOLDIER: Use your GPS here.

(KING WEREWOLF and SOLDIER go off in the car. They get to the cave.)

SOLDIER: Here it is sir! Have fun, don't kill yourself!

(KING WEREWOLF goes into the cave and puts his crown on the rock. KING VAMPIRE starts to push a big rock onto him. He calls to KING ZOMBIE.)

KING VAMPIRE: A little help here!?!

KING ZOMBIE: What? I'm gonna break my hand. I once broke my ear because you bit me.

KING VAMPIRE: Not my fault you taste like meat. Forget about it—just help me.

KING ZOMBIE: Fine, if I break my hand you pay me.

(KING WEREWOLF walks away before the rock falls. The rock bounces back and hits KING ZOMBIE's head off. KING ZOMBIE puts it back on.)

KING ZOMBIE: When we finish with him I'm going to finish you.

KING VAMPIRE: Sorry, it's not my fault it bounced back.

KING WEREWOLF: There's the diamond. I hope I got the right diamond.

(He gets the diamond and is about to leave.)

KING ZOMBIE: Oh no he got the diamond, we have no choice we have to kill him.

(KING VAMPIRE and KING ZOMBIE jump in front of KING WEREWOLF.)

KING WEREWOLF: What are you doing here?

KING VAMPIRE: To get revenge.

KING ZOMBIE: Let me do the talking, idiot.

KING VAMPIRE: Uh … King Zombie.

KING ZOMBIE: Stop interrupting me.

KING VAMPIRE: But…

KING ZOMBIE: No buts.

WEIRD SOUND: 5… 4… 3… 2… 1.

KING VAMPIRE: I'm trying to say that the King Werewolf escaped and in 5 seconds we're going to be trapped here forever.

KING ZOMBIE: Oh.

(When KING WEREWOLF runs he stops and swallows the diamond.)

KING WEREWOLF: Whoa that hurts, okay now I'm going home.

(Five minutes later.)

KING WEREWOLF: Okay I'm home, now where's that soldier so I could cut his neck out.

End of Play

The Adventures of the Amazing Wolf

by Finalist Vanessa Brotsky

Characters:
MAX
KATY
SNAPPY
LICORICE WITCH
AMAZING WOLF

SCENE:

MAX: My name is Max. I've heard of the Amazing Wolf that can grant anyone's wishes! I really want to go. I'm gonna ask Katy the bunny and Snappy the fox if they want to go. *(Runs offstage to get friends)*

(Gets friends and runs onstage.)

MAX: Hey Katy, hey Snappy. Do you want to come with me to see the Amazing Wolf? We have to go to Ice Cream Land.

KATY: What's the Amazing Wolf?

SNAPPY: I've heard of it before. It's a wolf that can grant any wish.

MAX: Exactly. So do you want to come or what?

KATY and SNAPPY: Okay!

MAX: But we have to watch out for the Witch of Licorice!

ALL: *(Singing)* We're on our way to Ice Cream Land, Ice Cream Ice Cream Land!

KATY: Oh my gosh! What is that thing?!?

SNAPPY: Oh no! It's the Licorice Witch!

(SNAPPY hugs MAX and KATY.)

MAX: *(Whispering)* It's okay. We can try to stay away from her.

KATY: Okay, let's do this.

(They start walking some more.)

LICORICE WITCH: Hahahaha! You think you can get away from me?! *(Stomps hard)* I have heard your whole little plan hahahaha!

MAX: I think we better be going.

LICORICE WITCH: Oh no you don't!

(KATY, SNAPPY and MAX run away from LICORICE WITCH. LICORICE WITCH checks watch.)

LICORICE WITCH: (Screaming) Oh great I'm late! I'm not done with you!

MAX: (Pointing) Oh look I can see the Amazing Wolf's hut from here.

SNAPPY: Cool!

KATY: Let's go.

(They all walk.)

MAX: Okay, okay. This is it.

(MAX smiles. They all get close to the door.)

LICORICE WITCH: Hey, stop right there. I said I would be back, right?

(They all take a step back with fear.)

SNAPPY: I guess so.

MAX: (Whispers) Watch this. (Normal voice) Hey Witch, go away or I— I— I will…

LICORICE WITCH: Whatcha gonna do about it? Because I'm gonna take you three as slaves!

(SNAPPY and KATY run behind the bush. MAX takes out potion and puts it on LICORICE WITCH.)

LICORICE WITCH: Oh no! I'm disappearing!

(WITCH disappears. MAX, KATY and SNAPPY run into hut.)

AMAZING WOLF: Who's here!?!

MAX: We want our wishes granted.

AMAZING WOLF: Okay, think your wishes and they will come true.

(They all think.)

MAX, KATY and SNAPPY: (In unison) Ready!

AMAZING WOLF: Your wishes come true! Here, Snappy. (Hands keys to SNAPPY) There's a red car waiting for you.

SNAPPY: Yay! (Runs to the car)

AMAZING WOLF: Here, Katy. Your wish for world peace came true!

KATY: Yay! *(Runs to the car)*

AMAZING WOLF: Oh! And Max. I did not forget about you. Here is your pet. Here's a dog.

MAX: Yay! *(Runs to the car with dog. They all drive away, happily ever after.)*

End of Play

The Chest of Money

by Finalist Stefan Ivanoui

Characters:
JACK
FLY SPY
SKUNK POLICEMAN
SHARK
BLACKBEARD
NARRATOR
MINIONS

SCENE 1:

(JACK is in his house looking at his picture of him and his brother BLACKBEARD.)

JACK: Hi my name is Jack and I like to go treasure hunting and so does my brother but he got evil because when we were kids my dad Hector brought a treasure box full of treasure and he said you boys will have to fight to see who wins and gets the treasure for himself.

(They fight. JACK wins. BLACKBEARD is mad. He leaves.)

JACK: Bye brother. I'm sorry that you lost.

That's the story about me and my brother. And nowadays I live with my dog. And with my wife. I am also a pirate, and so was my brother. *(Whispers to the audience)* I have a secret to tell and you can't tell nobody about it. I found a treasure map on my brother's territory, and yes I found my brother after ten years. I never saw him ever since. I needed a good plan. So I went to find a crew to help me find the map for the treasure. And the perfect crew would be a Shark Pirate, a Skunk Policeman and the Fly Spy. I was thinking to get the Fly Spy because he is small and good to me, he is also good to get into small places. I need him to get in the prison for the Skunk. The place where I can find him is in a swamp, so I have to go.

(JACK takes his ship and sails away.)

SCENE 2:

JACK: There he is. I need your help Fly Spy to infiltrate the prison. Will you help me Fly Spy?

FLY SPY: Okay, I will help you Jack. But, you need to do me a favor. I need you to help me free my brother from Blackbeard.

JACK: Blackbeard! That is my brother!

FLY SPY: He is your brother! OMG man! Okay I will help you.

JACK: Good, now we need to get in the prison to get the Skunk out to help us.

NARRATOR: So Jack and Fly Spy travel until they reach the prison.

SCENE 3:

JACK: We finally made it to the prison where the Skunk lives. Fly Spy go through the vent and open the front gate.

NARRATOR: Fly Spy went through the vent and he dodged blades in the air vent. He got to the control room and pushed the "open gate" button. Jack got in and saw the Skunk and climbed the tower to get him.

JACK: Skunk, I need your help.

SKUNK: I would help you, but my dad will not let me.

JACK: He is not going to get mad. Really.

SKUNK: Are you sure?

JACK: Yeah.

SKUNK: Okay I will help you.

JACK: Now we need to get Shark. He lives in the ocean. But we need a boat.

SKUNK: What I have one. We can get to the ocean.

NARRATOR: So Jack, Spy Fly and Skunk went to the ocean.

SCENE 4:

JACK: Well we are here. SHARK! SHARK! Where are you?

SHARK: What do you want?!

JACK: Well we need your help to get a treasure map that is hidden in Blackbeard's base.

SHARK: Blackbeard? No way man, he was terrible. Get out of here! But—get out of here!!

FLY SPY and SKUNK: *(Both of them talk at the same time)* Well he is no help at all.

SKUNK: Let's get out of here.

NARRATOR: So they went to the camp of Blackbeard.

JACK: Let's go get the map.

SKUNK: Wait! Look your brother found the map.

FLY SPY: We should wait until night until they all go to sleep.

JACK: Good idea.

NARRATOR: Time passed and passed and it finally got night.

JACK: Now we should get the map.

FLY SPY and SKUNK: Let's go.

JACK: Let's split up, we can find it faster.

NARRATOR: They searched and searched all night and finally they found it.

JACK: I found it. Let's go to my ship and get the treasure.

NARRATOR: They were walking slowly to not wake up nobody. But, finally Blackbeard heard footsteps and woke up.

BLACKBEARD: Is that you Jack?! Get them my minions.

MINIONS: Okay.

NARRATOR: Jack and the others started running and running and got on the ship.

JACK: The treasure map says we have to get to an island in the Pacific Ocean.

FLY SPY and SKUNK: Yes sir.

JACK: Faster! Faster people!

BLACKBEARD: Get them!

NARRATOR: Blackbeard and his minions got on the ship and went after them.

JACK: Anything?

SKUNK: No sir.

FLY SPY: There it is.

JACK: Okay.

BLACKBEARD: Come on, come on you guys. Faster, we are catching up to them.

JACK: We are looking for an upside down tree.

SKUNK: I found it.

JACK: Great, start digging... I got it.

BLACKBEARD: Not so fast, you guys think you can get the map from me and the treasure when I'm sleeping.

JACK: Yes, we thought we can.

BLACKBEARD: My minions get them and the treasure out of the ground. Also get the map and my brother and his helpers.

MINIONS: Yes sir.

NARRATOR: Blackbeard took him on his ship and made them walk the plank.

BLACKBEARD: Okay, walk the plank to your doom or be my prisoner. Choose now or say goodbye to your friends.

JACK: I choose the plank.

SKUNK and FLY SPY: Don't choose that. You want to die?

BLACKBEARD: Move!

NARRATOR: Jack jumped and grabbed onto the side of the plank. Blackbeard thought he had died and so did his helpers. Jack was watching for him to move onto another place on the ship.

BLACKBEARD: Push the other into the shark's mouth.

(From nowhere comes JACK to help. From nowhere comes SHARK to help them get back on the ship. BLACKBEARD looks around.)

BLACKBEARD: You are alive?!

JACK: Attack you guys! Cover me and I will take care of my brother.

NARRATOR: Blackbeard went to the top of the ship and Jack followed him.

JACK: Why must we fight brother?

BLACKBEARD: It's because you won the fight when we were kids.

JACK: Wait I have an idea!

BLACKBEARD: What?

JACK: We can share the treasure half and half.

BLACKBEARD: Okay, brother.

JACK: Here, you get your half and I get my half.

NARRATOR: And so forth, Blackbeard lived with Jack and lived forever.

End of Play

Runny Babbit

by Finalist Karla Rodriguez

Characters:
ANABELL
UMANUEL
GARDENER
MANAGER

INTRODUCTION:

ANABELL: Hi, my name is Anabell and I'm a bunny rabbit. I loooove carrots but it is difficult to find a carrot. By the way, did you know I live in a forest full of volcanoes and trees? There is a man that wants to dig them all up but he won't find any because I eat most of them.

UMANUEL: Hello, I don't think you know my name. If you do know my name, good for you. If you don't know, well, my name is Chuky and my secret is that I don't really like animals.

SCENE 1:

ANABELL: *(Digging)* I'm hungry and haven't found a single carrot.

UMANUEL: So let me see, *(Looking at his plans)* I'm going to dig up all the carrots there are in this forest.

ANABELL: *(Screaming in hunger)* I'm soooo hungry, I think that I will die if I don't have at least one carrot.

UMANUEL: Well I don't think I have to dig all the carrots up because Anabell ate them all up.

SCENE 2:

ANABELL: *(Digging then stops because she finds a garden full of fruit)* Wow, a place full of goodies.

GARDENER: *(Looking at ANABELL)* Hey you! Shu, shu, shu!!! Go away!

ANABELL: Seriously, not even a single bit of lettuce?

GARDENER: NO! Rabbits and other animals are not allowed in my garden.

UMANUEL: Now what am I going to do? I don't have any carrots.

MANAGER: Umanuel you are fired!!!

UMANUEL: NO!!! Why!!!

ANABELL: Yes I did it, now I will have carrots ... but where will I get them?

GARDENER: I can give you some of my carrots from the garden.

ANABELL: Really!

GARDENER: Yes.

ANABELL: Okay I won't die of hunger.

End of Play

Eliza's Journey

by Finalist Phoebe Snow

Characters:
ELIZA
CHRYSANTHEMUM
GARTH
LUCY
CECIEL
MYSTERY CAT

SCENE 1: Introduction.

(ELIZA, a cat, is running through the forest.)

ELIZA: *(Crying)* Why did this *(Sniff)* happen? *(Sobbing)*

(A new cat, CHRYSANTHEMUM, stops her.)

CHRYSANTHEMUM: What's wrong?

ELIZA: *(Sobs)* My mother died and I am running away. She was the only one who took care of me there. *(Sniff)* She gave me her ruby necklace when she died. *(ELIZA cleans herself up.)*

CHRYSANTHEMUM: *(Sympathetic)* How did she die?

ELIZA: *(Angry)* She was murdered. *(Bitterly)* I'm sure Ceciel made it so, probably sent one of her trusted cats to kill her.

CHRYSANTHEMUM: I'll be your friend and I'll stick with you the whole time through bad times. Now let's go meet the cats that live here.

(The two cats walk offstage. The two cats walk into a village.)

CHRYSANTHEMUM: Hello everyone, I brought a new edition to the group. Her name is Eliza.

GARTH: Welcome Eliza. I am Garth, the leader of this humble group.

ELIZA: *(Blushes)* Hi Garth. I am happy to be here. *(Smiles)*

GARTH: *(Blushes a little)* Well good. Lucy, Chrysanthemum, will you show her the way around the camp?

(After the tour.)

LUCY: So that is the camp.

ELIZA: Wow you guys have a really great camp.

CHRYSANTHEMUM: Yeah everybody pitches in to take care of the camp.

ELIZA: I think I will try and meet all the cats here before sundown. I'll also try and see exactly how things work.

(CECIEL watches through the bushes.)

CECIEL: There there my little spy, do my bidding.

(MYSTERY CAT walks close by in shadows.)

MYSTERY CAT: I am her friend now, she trusts me. I will bring her to you.

CECIEL: (Smiles) Gooooood.

(MYSTERY CAT slinks off.)

SCENE 2:

ELIZA: So I met everyone and I caught a mouse to add to the pile of food.

LUCY: You're so kind. Thanks. The fresh-kill pile is over there.

CHRYSANTHEMUM: Or you could eat it or share it with someone.

ELIZA: No I'm fine, I'll put it in the pile.

LUCY: After you're done I want you to meet Garth's sister, just you and me.

SCENE 3:

(ELIZA follows LUCY into a dark cave with water dripping from ceiling.)

ELIZA: Wow it's really dark in here. Are you sure she lives here?

LUCY: It gets lighter up ahead.

(Two cats close the exit.)

CECIEL: Lucy thank you for bringing her to me. Now we fight. I win, you die.

ELIZA: Lucy how could you do this to me!

LUCY: (Snobbish) Sorry, I am loyal to Ceciel.

(CHRYSANTHEMUM runs in with GARTH and lots of other cats.)

GARTH: Sister you are an abomination. I banish you.

(CECIEL runs off and her cats follow her.)

108

GARTH: I think that you deserve to be leader. You are aware of lots of things. Would you like to be leader with me?

ELIZA: Yes oh yes. I will rule with you.

End of Play

The Wicked Witch of the West

by Finalist Arnasia Vaughn

Characters:
EMMA
CHRISTE
JACK
SERENA

SCENE:

EMMA: *(Sighs)* Hi everybody, my name is Emma. I'm not having a very good day as you can see. I can't find the diamond that controls the kingdom, if that gets in the wrong hands our world will be destroyed—it will lose color. Let me try to call Dad, you know, the king. Oh I forgot he left it in the castle, I don't know where he is. I guess I will have to get the diamond myself. But that is really weird, the diamond can't just get up and walk out by itself—someone took it and I'm going to find out who. Today my dad called me but it wasn't on his phone, he always calls me on his phone but last night I heard someone walking around the castle. My dad wasn't here, the servants weren't here either—my father said they could get a day off. I was in the castle alone but I don't think I was alone. Christe, Jack, I'm over here. I found some information about a witch that was eager to get her hands on a diamond but in the book it didn't say what diamond she wanted. I think she stole the diamond but I'm really not sure, but I am going to find out.

(At the castle.)

EMMA: Hey Christe, Jack, today I found some information about some witch. I think she is the Wicked Witch of the West, I mean of our west. She loves diamonds, maybe she loves diamonds that control the kingdom.

CHRISTE: Wait wait, so you telling me that there's a witch.

EMMA: I think I've been telling you that for the last five minutes, can you comprehend because I know I can!!

JACK: Emma will you just stop, maybe she don't believe because I really don't think there's a witch, she would've been took the diamond right?

EMMA: There is one, I'm not lying I promise, she waits for the right time. *(Whisper)* She comes when the portal opens from the underworld. She has been defeated. She comes on Halloween.

JACK: Wow you just don't make any sense. You lost your diamond on October 3. It is October 29.

EMMA: But, she did take it, I think she was the one who killed my mom, my dad said it was the dark one!

CHRISTE: I'm sorry about your mom but this witch thing is not really making sense right now. Bye guys see ya later.

JACK: Christe wait! I'm coming with you. Sorry Emma but I just don't believe you.

(At the castle.)

EMMA: *(Sighs)* I really need to call my sister, dangit I forgot her number. I think Dad got it in the phone book, let me go check. I wish I had magic to make it appear, I don't like to walk around in here alone, I usually have servants. I'll go get the phone number. Let me look in here, bingo found it here it is.

(Calling SERENA.)

SERENA: Hello. Who is this?

EMMA: *(Crying)* It's me, Emma.

SERENA: Hey, hey Emma why are you calling me so late?

EMMA: It is an emergency. Can you come to the castle please?

SERENA: Okay I'll be over there in two minutes.

EMMA: Please be careful please, okay.

SERENA: Okay, okay just open the gates.

(SERENA beeps the horn.)

SERENA: Emma I'm here, open the gates.

EMMA: I'm right here. We can't go in the castle there's something in there!

SERENA: Where's Dad, where is he? Emma start talking.

EMMA: It's a long story, I will have to tell you a little bit later. Okay some witch took the diamond that controls the kingdom and Dad, I just don't know where he is!

SERENA: How do you know a witch took it b—

EMMA: I don't know but I'm going to find out.

SERENA: We look for Dad last. I really don't want him up my back right now!

EMMA: Okay!!

(Walking in the woods.)

SERENA: Where is the witch?

EMMA: In the book I read it said she waits on Halloween to come out of the portal. I'll tell you about that later.

SERENA: Where is the portal?

EMMA: The portal is in the enchanted forest, but we need protection—that forest is full of surprises.

SERENA: What do you mean full of surprises?

EMMA: It has booby traps.

SERENA: NO, NO I'm not going in that forest, I'm sorry.

EMMA: Fine I'll go by myself.

SERENA: *(Running)* Emma, Emma wait. I'll go with you, but do you have any friends?

EMMA: Yeah! But they really don't want to get into this witch thing.

SERENA: Yes they will, I have a plan!

EMMA: Okay! Their names are Jack and Christe.

SERENA: Okay, let's go get them. Where do they live?

EMMA: Right through there. Jack is at Christe's house. So, what did you mean when you said you don't want Dad up your back?

SERENA: When I was 17 years old I got married to a man named Prince John, but Dad didn't really like him but I told Dad that I really didn't care what he thought about him.

EMMA: But why did you have to leave me, we were really close back then.

SERENA: I'm sorry Emma but I had to have a life too. I was like a servant to him. I couldn't take it anymore.

EMMA: You didn't even come to Mom's funeral.

SERENA: Queen Ally wasn't my mom—Queen Sebrena was, my mom died when I was born, she had a stroke when she was having me.

EMMA: We have a lot in common then, both of our moms died when we were a baby, we don't get along with Dad so much.

SERENA: Yeah, I think we do.

EMMA: Are we here yet?

SERENA: Yes we are. *(Beeps the horn.)*

JACK: Hey Emma. What are you doing here?

(Walking to the café.)

EMMA: I know you don't believe me about that witch but me and my sister can't go alone. Will you help me?

CHRISTE: Sure why not!

JACK: Yes I'm in.

CHRISTE: But me and Jack have something to tell you.

EMMA: What, you can tell me anything.

JACK: Me and Christe...

CHRISTE: We like each other!!!

EMMA: So how long have you two been dating?

JACK: For three months.

EMMA: Christe can I talk to you for a minute please?

CHRISTE: Sure!

EMMA: You know that I liked Jack.

CHRISTE: I don't care I did too, and anyway you didn't make a move.

EMMA: I was going to make a move when we got the diamond back.

CHRISTE: I will break up with him if you want me to.

EMMA: You can be happy and anyway, I don't need a boy in my life right now.

CHRISTE: Okay. Let's go kick some butt!

EMMA: Let's go.

SERENA: Are you guys ready?

BOTH: Yeah!

SERENA: Do you see that over there? It is something shiny.

EMMA: Wait do not go over there.

JACK: I'm going over there.

EMMA: Okay. Don't say I told you so.

SERENA: That's that witch.

EMMA: Are you sure?

SERENA: Yeah, who do you see walking around here with a robe on their head?

JACK: That's not a robe.

SERENA: Then what is it?

To be continued...

Wish for Light

by Finalist Anderson Waltz

Characters:
LAUREN
QUEEN

SCENE 1:

LAUREN: I want my world to change a lot! That's all I am asking for, the Sun! Nothing grows here, nothing is happy! Why can't the Queen bring back the Sun? It was here once, why'd she make it go away?! She, she ... is confusing, the things she does, the way she does them. Maybe I could ask her someday, why she won't bring the Sun—or if she even can.

QUEEN: *(British accent)* I'm the Queen, and I want to stay alive. You would <u>think</u> that would be a pretty popular wish, but here's the catch. I was cursed as a child that if light would fill my heart, if I shall be happy, satisfied, I shall die. So I spend my days being a lonely old lady sulking in her huge castle about her horrible, awful, no-good life.

SCENE 2: Lauren's room (in her house).

(LAUREN snaps.)

LAUREN: I bet I could write the Queen a letter and walk it to her castle. *(She starts writing.)* And, done. Now I just gotta walk it to the castle.

(LAUREN walks to castle and slips it in the "mailbox," which is the floor. QUEEN picks up letter.)

QUEEN: What is this?! *(Reads paper)* Why I <u>have</u> to fix this, now.

(QUEEN walks to LAUREN's home. Knocks on door. LAUREN answers door.)

LAUREN: Hullo yer Majesty, what do you need?

QUEEN: Are you Lauren?

LAUREN: *(Sarcastically)* Um... I think so.

QUEEN: Not funny dear. Now, child, I read your letter, and it's very, interesting ... and I have many questions for you to answer for me.

LAUREN: Like, what questions?

QUEEN: First off, why do you want me to change?!

LAUREN: Well—

QUEEN: I mean, isn't it perfect here? Don't answer me, because it is. And you are not going to keep up this foolishness of bringing back the sun. Because it is gone. Now, I hope I don't have to confront your little face again!

(QUEEN walks away.)

LAUREN: *(To herself)* Sheesh! *(Mockingly)* But yeah, like I'm gonna stop because she told me to. *(Still to herself)* So... Now the Queen's onto me... I <u>have</u> to think of a plan. Hmmm... Maybe the library has something! Or maybe— no not the internet, library it is! This is perfect, the library is practically my neighbor! A block away, just perfect!

(LAUREN walks to library and picks up a book.)

LAUREN: Wow this is <u>old</u>! *(Blows off the book like it is very dusty)* Whoa— *(COUGH!)* Hmm... So-lar Sys ... tems! I think this book is the one. *(Flips through pages)* Blah-blah Venus, blah-blah Saturn... Here! Sun. *(Reads through very interested)* Well, I think I am <u>so</u> going to check this out!

(LAUREN walks home with book in hand.)

LAUREN: Now, here comes the hard part: tricking the Queen.

(Walks off.)

<u>SCENE 3</u>: *The Queen's throne room, QUEEN sitting on throne.*

QUEEN: I'm so BORE-D. But all I can think about is that little <u>brat</u> Lauren! Like who needs that orange lightbulb in the sky!? Like—

(Knock on the door. QUEEN answers door. LAUREN is at the door with a teapot in her hand.)

LAUREN: Hullo yer Majesty—

QUEEN: What do you want.

LAUREN: I would like to come to your castle to apologize over tea. *(Holds up teapot)*

QUEEN: No thank you.

LAUREN: Pleeeeeease?!

QUEEN: Fine, whatever.

(LAUREN sits down and pours tea.)

LAUREN: Why, you could never guess how much I want to apologize to you for being such a rebel to your perfect world.

QUEEN: *(Proudly)* Well it *is* perfect.

LAUREN: But you know, I've <u>always</u> wanted to see the genius wand that made this perfect place happen.

116

QUEEN: Well, it's kinda confidential...

LAUREN: Pul-eeese! It's been my all-time dream to see my #1 role model's wand.

QUEEN: OK, fine. I guess, it won't, hurt.

LAUREN: YAY!

(LAUREN and QUEEN walk to wand.)

QUEEN: *(Proudly)* Here it is.

(LAUREN runs to wand and takes it and runs outside.)

QUEEN: Noo, foolish child what are you doing!

LAUREN: I'm bringing back the Sun.

QUEEN: But, but, I will die.

LAUREN: Trust me, you won't. *(LAUREN points the wand to the sky and yells.)* My one wish, to bring back the Sun!

(Flash of light, and Sun appears. QUEEN starts to glow.)

QUEEN: What, what's happening!? I'm, I'm, not dead. What?! I feel, happy. Thank you child, for giving me my life back, my smile. And thank you for making this a perfect world.

LAUREN: Now we can grow things and we can have fun, and we can have daylight, we can have everything we ever wanted. Happiness included, especially for the Queen.

QUEEN: I have my life back! My happy my smile! My everything. All thanks to that smart, happy, amazing, wonderful Lauren.

End of Play

Untitled

by Finalist Kamarian Watkins

Characters:
PHIL
UNCLE MAGEE

SCENE 1:

PHIL: Hi, my name is Phil, Phil MaGee, and I'm the King of the Earth from this quest I took when I was in college so about *(High pitched voice)* a year ago and I have powers also and that King stuff and me having powers doesn't make me special, I'm still a regular person. And for the King stuff *(Takes a breath)* to go on I need a son and maybe a girl but let's get to the point. I have a girlfriend but in order to have a son and daughter I have to get married but there is one problem: my uncle Uncle MaGee says I'm too young to get married and blah blah and I'm like, "Dude I'm twenty-two I'm a grown man and I can make my own choices." *(Sighs)* Oh my god. *(In an upset voice)* Here we go he is coming. *(In a loud voice)* Hey.

UNCLE MAGEE: What's been going on, nothing? Are you still getting married?

PHIL: Yeah.

UNCLE MAGEE: But you're too young.

PHIL: I am twenty-two.

UNCLE MAGEE: But you are too young.

PHIL: Blah blah blah look I am not a little kid anymore.

UNCLE MAGEE: Alright you impressed me, you can get married now. You can get married.

To be continued...

Untitled

by Finalist Maiya Bryant

Characters:
ANNA
KATY
MARLEN
JOSH
MAN

ACT I, SCENE 1:

ANNA: My name's Anna. I'm 22 years old and live in Texas. My hair's dark brown and my eyes are kind of green-colored. I work at a 24/7 open diner called "Faith's Food" because I love to cook. That's why I have really big dreams of opening my own restaurant one day in NYC, hopefully. But until then, I'm just another girl with big dreams.

KATY: I'm Katy. My hair's red and I have brown eyes and freckles. I'm 22 and the ex-best friend of Anna. We were like sisters. We did everything together. Partied, hung out, everything. But our relationship drifted apart when I always wanted to go out and have fun, and she wanted to stay home, read her cooking book and try stupid recipes. I know, boring right? So we just drifted apart. I hung out with different people, she hung out with different people and we started not to like each other. She's always blurting out how she wants to be a "famous chef" but as long as I'm around, she won't.

MARLEN: Table 8 needs a new plate of special 3. It fell.

(ANNA takes her apron off and lays it on the table.)

ANNA: Sorry Mar. My shift is finally over and I am going home. But Taylor's coming in a few.

(ANNA waves bye to MARLEN before opening the back door to the kitchen and walking out, into the dark world.)

ANNA: *(Mumbles)* Oh gosh.

(ANNA sees KATY and a group of her old friends. She has no choice but to walk past them.)

JOSH: Well hello Anna.

(He puts his arm around her but she moves away.)

ANNA: *(Mumbles)* Hey.

(ANNA avoids looking at KATY as KATY stares at her with narrowed eyes. ANNA just looks at the ground.)

KATY: We were about to go to this party down the street. Why don't you come?

ANNA: Sorry. I gotta get home. *(She begins to walk away.)*

KATY: Let me guess. To cook? *(All the friends laugh. Even KATY. She yells to ANNA.)* You know you never gonna make it big, right? You're just gonna be another nobody just like your dad.

(ANNA counts to 10 in her head and ignores all the rude comments they are making about her. When ANNA looks back, she sees KATY staring back at her with a sympathetic look.)

ACT I, SCENE 2: The next day.

MARLEN: I need a new special 4 for table 2. *(Whines)* The baby knocked it off the table.

(ANNA gets up from her seat and sighs because she's having a bad day.)

ANNA: *(Mumbles)* Okay...

(MARLEN looks at her with a concerned look.)

MARLEN: What's wrong sweetie? You look sad today.

(ANNA puts on a fake smile.)

ANNA: Don't worry. I'm fine.

ACT I, SCENE 3: Hours later.

(ANNA starts cleaning the dishes because her shift is almost over. MARLEN calls, getting her attention.)

MARLEN: Anna!

(ANNA turns around.)

ANNA: No Mar... My shift is about over and I'm not staying any longer.

(MARLEN rolls her eyes.)

MARLEN: Actually, I wasn't going to ask you to stay. *(ANNA looks shocked. Playfully)* I was going to tell you that this man at table 12 wants to see you.

(ANNA looks confused.)

ANNA: Me? Why?

MARLEN: I don't know. All he said was, "May I speak to the chef?" And you. Are. The chef! Now go.

(MARLEN walks into the kitchen and pushes ANNA out. ANNA glares at MARLEN.)

ANNA: Can I help you sir?

MAN: Are you the woman who made this? *(He points at the food and ANNA smiles.)*

ANNA: Yes sir, I am.

MAN: Well that's good because I'm looking for a new chef for my restaurant, Schics.

(ANNA looks confused.)

ANNA: I'm sorry sir but I never heard of your restaurant.

MAN: You haven't because it's in NYC and I'm looking for a new chef.

(ANNA's eyes widen.)

MAN: Would you consider bec—

(ANNA cuts him off.)

ANNA: (Yells) Yes, yes, yes! I'll do it!

(Everyone in the place looks at her. MARLEN claps her hands.)

MAN: Great. Here's my card. Call me later tonight and we'll talk.

(MAN drops a stack of money on the table and leaves. MARLEN runs over to ANNA and hugs her.)

MARLEN: Oh my god! I'm so happy for you Anna! You're finally going to live your dream.

ANNA: I know! I'm so h—

(KATY runs by ANNA and pushes her as she runs out the doors.)

ANNA: I'll be back in a moment. (ANNA walks out of the building to find KATY crying on the stairs. ANNA runs to her.) Are you okay Katy?

KATY: Do I look okay to you?

(ANNA sits next to her and pats her back but KATY shoos it away.)

ANNA: What's wrong? Did I do something?

KATY: Yes. Yes you did.

ANNA: What did I do?

KATY: Everything! First you find your own group of friends and leave me alone! I had to find new friends because you acted like I was a ghost! And now you're leaving! Out of 18 years of being friends, you're leaving me! Why do you always do this to me? (KATY lays her head on ANNA's shoulder and cries.)

ANNA: I didn't realize that I did that. I felt like you were drifting away from me.

KATY: Only because you were off getting your life together and becoming something! When I'm just a farm girl! I felt like I was a burden on you!

ANNA: You were not and will never be a burden on me! You're like my sister and I love you so much!

(KATY wipes her eyes and looks up at ANNA.)

KATY: Still?

(ANNA smiles.)

ANNA: Still.

(KATY lays her head on ANNA's shoulder again.)

KATY: I'm going to miss you a lot when you leave, Anna. Promise you won't forget me and you'll always call.

(ANNA puts her thumb on KATY's and pinky promises.)

ANNA: I promise.

End of Play

Untitled

by Finalist Emily Deutchman (with assistance from Gracie Cabral)

Characters:
JOEY
BANKY DOLLAR
AMBER
MR. PAPER CLIP MAN
JAKE FROM STATE FARM

SCENE 1:

JOEY: Hi, my name is Joey. So, guess what happened today? I was walking along a sidewalk with my favorite pig, Oink, and this large man who called himself Banky Dollar said he had to take my farm away. But you're probably thinking what, who, where, etc. OK so let me back myself up. As I said before, I'm Joey. I live in Iowa on a big farm with my four horses, six pigs, two chickens, and 18 cows. Yep I said it: 18. On top of that I have a mom, a dad, and me (I'm a only child). So let me tell you more about Banky.

BANKY DOLLAR: Hi em yemm ahh ugg yemm, sorry, don't mind my best friend Mr. Cake. OK so now MEEE. I am the amazing, wonderful, handsome, (skinny) Banky Dollar! So you see I work at a bank (ironic right) and as a banker. I see money every day but it's so sad cuz I am poor. So here's what's great. I found this farm and this horrible boy named Joey. He and his family have a farm. Anyway I want it, and my best cousin ever is Mr. Paper Clip Man. He's going to blow up the world with trees. So yeah, bye.

SCENE 2:

JOEY: Oh, hi. What are you doing hiding behind my pig?

AMBER: Oh, because I ran away.

JOEY: From who?

AMBER: This creepy guy named the Paper Clip Man. He doesn't like it when I call him creepy. But I call him creepy anyways.

JOEY: Oh. Why were you running away from him?

AMBER: Because he chased me out of his secret lair made out of paper clips and it's also full of paper clips with a wooden bomb.

JOEY: Oh, that's nice. Ohhh wait ... wait... Have I seen Paper Clip Man before, or someone like him?

AMBER: You must be thinking about his cousin, Banky Dollar. My friend, Jake from State Farm told me. He's a hippo.

JOEY: Oh, cool. Yeah I know Mr. Banky Dollar. He tried to steal my farm away! We should do something about it.

125

AMBER: Yeah, maybe.

JOEY: Well, OK, so we want to stop that Paper Clip Man from blowing up the world with a wooden bomb. And we also want to stop Mr. Banky Dollar from taking my farm away. How should we do that? Wait, I kinda have to go though. Maybe we can talk about it some other time?

AMBER: Yeah, but can I just ask you one question?

JOEY: Sure.

AMBER: It doesn't make any sense. Why would the Paper Clip Man want to blow up the world and Banky Dollar want to take your farm, cuz the farm's just gonna blow up when the Paper Clip Man blows up the world?

JOEY: I have no idea. Maybe you should ask my fourth pig, Robert. He's pretty smart.

AMBER: OK, I will so "do that."

JOEY: Alright, gotta go. Bye!

AMBER: See ya!

SCENE 3:

JOEY: Oh thank God I made it here! My mom started getting really mad at me because I was running a lot, trying to find time to meet with you.

AMBER: Yeah, I understand. But the real problem is the Paper Clip Man keeps on expanding his lair made of paper clips, cuz I keep on accidentally knocking it over. OK, maybe not by accident. But I keep on knocking it over.

JOEY: Well, maybe he's trying to fit some giant bomb in it and make some bigger excuse about it.

AMBER: Uh, yeah. Let me tell you one little thing. Um, I'm not sure if this is the exact number, but there were about, like, a lot of trees, like let's say 500. Now there are about 200 ... 300.

JOEY: So there's less trees?

AMBER: Yes. The thing is, since bombs are so expensive, he's trying to make it easier to make them by cutting down trees cuz there are a lot of trees and then apparently he has this machine—I don't know what it's called—Jake from State Farm wouldn't talk about that ... anyways, so he turns the trees that he cut down into bombs.

JOEY: OK, first of all, that is very bad for the environment! And second of all, I like my farm! I want to keep my farm. How can we stop Banky Dollar and Paper Clip Man?

AMBER: Well, here's an idea. How about we make them fight over something, and then when one of them is arguing or something, we sneak in and then take away the giant machine thingy that makes the bombs, and then we give Banky Dollar three pieces of bacon to not take your farm?

JOEY: OK, first of all, we could use Jake from State Farm to come in and fight with Mr. Paper Clip Man, so me and you can sneak in with your awesome dog smells and take the bomb thing away? And, we can give Mr. Banky Dollar a little bit of money from my thing or we can blow him up … with cake!

AMBER: Yeah, that's a good idea! Cuz Jake from State Farm could be mocking the Paper Clip Man by getting up on his knees and pretending he's fat and acting like Banky Dollar, and then he copies whatever Banky Dollar says. And then Paper Clip Man also gets mad and then we sneak in!

JOEY: That works pretty well. But by the way, this plan is really stupid because I'm only like 7 and you're a dog.

AMBER: Well, yeah, good point.

JOEY: And another problem—Jake from State Farm, he's in California right now. Why did he have to go to Disney?!

AMBER: I don't know. But I think I could contact him because he's been trying to make this thing called a jet pack and he gave me one and he says I have to test it before he comes back. So I can fly to California with this "jet pack" and then I can tell him to go back and then I can leave!

JOEY: OK, that plan sounds really good. OK, so let me just straighten it out—we are going to fly to California with a jet pack and pick up Jake from State Farm, bring him back here, make him distract Mr. Paper Clip Man while we go in there and take his bomb thing and blow it up with his other bomb thing so then all the bombs blow up? And then we're going to take a bunch of cake and take the other bomb thing and blow up Banky Dollar with the cake and the other bomb! And then they'll both be gone! And we will win the world! Right?

AMBER: Yeah. Sure.

JOEY: Alright! I gotta go buy a jet pack. Bye!

AMBER: See ya! But you do know I have like 50 somewhere hidden in the forest, and I think one of the trees was cut down, so Banky Dollar and the Paper Clip Man might have like 50 jet packs in a tree that they're about to put in a bomb machine?

JOEY: Well I own a farm and I have a giant bank in my backyard—TMI—that's why Banky Dollar likes me. And I can take that money to buy the jet packs. Now stop talking, my mouth is hurting. Bye!

AMBER: Bye!

SCENE 4:

JAKE FROM STATE FARM: Hello Paper Clip Man and Banky Dollar! How's it going? So, you wanna not be in the lair? OK, so I'll just knock the whole lair down. And knock it down cuz it's made out of paper clips. You should really get bricks or something else. Or maybe hay. I'm not sure. Why am I still talking?

JOEY: Come on, Amber! Let's go!

AMBER: OK! OK! Let's go! C'mon, hurry up!

JAKE FROM STATE FARM: Hey! Joey, Amber! This is really hard!

127

JOEY: Sorry. Just go over there and talk to Banky Dollar about cake and Paper Clip Man about the newest, improved paper clip.

JAKE FROM STATE FARM: OK! Hey Paper Clip Man and Banky Dollar! Hey Banky Dollar, there's this really awesome cake called the "Cake Cake." You should really try it out. And the Paper Clip Man—two things for you. First of all, there's this brand new thing called the "Paper Clip Paper Clip" where it's so amazing and it can never be bent. And it is amazing! And I found out that there are Martians on Mars! And I am totally not lying even though I sorta am. Anyways, Martians on Mars is totally real. And you should go to Mars straight away and not blow up Earth and then just check it out for yourself.

(While that is going on, this is going on too...)

JOEY: I got the bomb! I got it! Amber, come on! Hurry up! Let's run out of here!

AMBER: Suggestion—don't scream that!

MR. PAPER CLIP MAN: I got you now, kid!

JOEY: Oh no! Runnnnnn!

JAKE FROM STATE FARM: I'm running as fast as I can! A hippo does not have the best feet!

MR. PAPER CLIP MAN: You know you've been running for like a whole minute and you've gotten about one inch away from my lair.

BANKY DOLLAR: Mr. Paper Clip Man, I don't know how I am related to you. This is the most stupid plan ever! I'm leaving and taking this cake!

MR. PAPER CLIP MAN: For Pete's sake! You do realize that you can just steal stuff instead of having to take a boy's some sort of farm. You do realize when I blow up the world, your farm's gonna go "bye bye"!

BANKY DOLLAR: My farm is not gonna go "bye bye." I heard it's on a very specific plot of land that does not support tree blowup. And so does the rest of the world. By the way, trees do not make great bombs.

To be continued...

God Makes A Way

by Finalist Jaiden Fisher

Characters:
DARNELL
NARRATOR
FATHER
JAKE
MR. TOMAS
MOM
DR. MATTHEWS

ACT I, SCENE 1:

DARNELL: Hi my name is Darnell and when I was young I was abused by my father. I have a best friend that went to the same school with me but I didn't want to tell him that he was beating me. Reason why: I was scared. I didn't know what he was going to say. He might have told everyone about it and they might laugh or tease me. Now I'm in college. I'm 18 years old, on the varsity football team and captain. I live in New York City. My mom has cancer from smoking because of the stress my father put her through. Some of the things he did was cheat on my mom, beat my mom and beat me. Now I'm taking care of her and going to school. It's tough doing both of these things but I know I can do this.

ACT I, SCENE 2:

NARRATOR: Once upon a time there was a boy named Darnell. When he was young he was abused by his father.

(Door slams. Loud footsteps.)

FATHER: I told you to do your chores!

DARNELL: I had to do my homework. *(DARNELL is about to cry.)*

FATHER: You know what, I'm tired of talking.

DARNELL: No please!

(DARNELL's FATHER pulls out a charger cord and hits DARNELL on the back and leaves welts of blood on his back.)

DARNELL: *(To the audience)* I really want to tell Jake about my dad but I don't know what he's going to do, he might tell everyone at school then they will laugh and tease me. *(DARNELL walks away.)*

ACT I, SCENE 3: The next day at school.

(DARNELL walks in. He finds JAKE.)

JAKE: Hey Darnell, you ready?

DARNELL: Ready for what?

JAKE: The water balloon fight bruhh.

DARNELL: *(Forgetting the scars on his back)* That's today. Yeah I'm ready!

(Then comes time for the balloon fight.)

MR. TOMAS: All boys take off your shirts. All girls put T-shirts on, then meet me outside. *(DARNELL takes off his shirt. Everyone stops.)* What is that Mr. Smith?

DARNELL: What Mr. Tomas?

MR. TOMAS: Your back son. *(Then DARNELL remembers the scars. He feels embarrassed.)* Who did this to you.

DARNELL: My dad. *(He feels very ashamed.)*

JAKE: Why didn't you tell me? I'm your best friend.

DARNELL: Said sorry. *(DARNELL runs away.)*

ACT I, SCENE 4: 8 years later. Darnell is a football player, a straight-A student and captain of the team. Darnell's mother has cancer. He's the only person taking care of her.

JAKE: Heard about your mom, how's she doing?

DARNELL: She's hanging in.

JAKE: That's cool. I'm going to come over and help out.

DARNELL: Thanks man.

ACT I, SCENE 5: Later that day.

(Knocks on door.)

DARNELL: Who is it?

JAKE: It's me, Jake. Open up.

(Door opens.)

DARNELL: Sup.

MOM: Who's there?

JAKE: Hi Mrs. Smith.

MOM: *(Laughing)* Oh hi there Jake. Why are you here?

JAKE: Told Darnell that I would help out and talk about our football game tomorrow.

MOM: Okay don't be loud.

JAKE: I won't, I promise Mrs. Smith.

ACT I, SCENE 6: *Later that night.*

(DARNELL's MOM is having an asthma attack.)

MOM: *(Soft voice)* I can't breathe.

(DARNELL and JAKE hear strange noises coming from MOM's room. DARNELL wakes JAKE up.)

DARNELL: Something's wrong with Mom. Hurry come on!

JAKE: Okay! *(DARNELL and JAKE run upstairs.)*

DARNELL: Mom are you okay?!

JAKE: I'm calling the police.

DARNELL: Hurry please.

ACT I, SCENE 7: *At the hospital.*

JAKE: What happened?

DARNELL: I don't know.

JAKE: Well man I hope and pray your mom is okay.

DARNELL: Me too.

(DR. MATTHEWS comes out of the room.)

DR. MATTHEWS: There's something I need to tell you guys. Mrs. Smith has ... died.

JAKE and DARNELL: What!!! How!!!

DR. MATTHEWS: She had an asthma attack.

DARNELL: *(Talking under his breath)* First my dad now my mom, why is all of this happening to me? *(DARNELL cries.)*

DR. MATTHEWS: Did your mother have asthma when she was young?

DARNELL: Yes why? She said that it wasn't serious.

DR. MATTHEWS: Well over the years her asthma was deteriorating.

DARNELL: Why didn't she tell me? I thought that having cancer was enough.

DR. MATTHEWS: I think she didn't tell you because she had cancer and didn't want you to worry about two illnesses and for you to just worry about one of them. I think that you guys should go and settle at home.

DARNELL: We will Doc. *(DARNELL and JAKE leave the hospital.)*

ACT I, SCENE 8:

DARNELL: Hi, I want to tell you about how my life changed during this play. Since my mom died I finished college, went to law school, became a lawyer, and I'm a father to two beautiful children. I'm married and this shows that God can make a way out of no way. My life was filled with pain and embarrassment, but somehow I put all of that to the side and moved on and now I'm successful in life.

End of Play

Two Halves

by Finalist Shannya Judd

Characters:
BLUE
RED/???
SJ
KURO
DARK LORD/???

SCENE: Early after a long hard day at school filled with tests, work and detention, our normal high school protagonist BLUE gets home from school. Like every day when he gets home, he turns on the TV, but he finds Flame Fox News on TV instead of Pokémon. His house is on the TV with the title "Breaking News" along with the words that say, "Local neighborhood UFO sighting." Another one of Blue's house on the TV. Could it be true...?

BLUE: Wh-what the news can't be right! Every dumb house that I move into has some type of crazy story behind it! Maybe it's someone else's house... Th-that looks a lot ... like ... mine... Well! It's getting cold in here I need my axe looks like I need to go get some wood.

(BLUE walks out back to go cut down a tree to get some wood but then he sees some strange thing sticking out of the ground and drops his wood.)

BLUE: What the flim-flam! *(BLUE touches the thing slowly. To himself)* Is this what the UFO dropped off?

(BLUE starts to yell and scream from the poles of the thing sticking from out of the ground!!!)

BLUE: Guhaaaaaaaaa!!!

(BLUE falls to the ground from the pain and passes out.)

???: Hey you get up! Hello?! Are you dead. *(Poke poke poke)*

BLUE: *(Waking up from his painful rest)* Huh? What? Who are you?!

???: What the ohhh you didn't hear me?!

BLUE: What... NO! I was half dead for about—

???: An hour and a half...

BLUE: Just tell me who you are.

???: Well fine! My name is Red and I was sent here to partner up with you to *(Starts fake boxing)* fight evil so you won't plum-up and die.

BLUE: What makes you think I'm gonna die.

RED: I don't know because you're weak...

BLUE: I'm not weak! And I'm not falling for your dumb prank, "Red."

RED: What are you talking about, my name is Red!

BLUE: Fine then, what's your last name?!

RED: Um well... uh... Ya see I didn't have—

BLUE: Ah ha! You are a prankster!

RED: Guhaa! *(Picks BLUE up by the collar and fakes as if he's gonna punch BLUE in the face.)* Listen to me! I am not a liar and don't you ever call me one!!!

BLUE: Get off me. *(Swings at RED)*

(RED catches and holds BLUE's fist.)

BLUE: Rahhhh let go of me!!

(RED lets go and pushes him away. BLUE hits the tree really hard.)

BLUE: *(Hacks up blood)* H-how *(Hack)* d-did you do that!? *(Hack)*

RED: I told you, I'm from the Type A Domo Clan.

BLUE: *(Hack hack)* So... Your last name is Domo?

RED: Um... I guess so...

BLUE: *(Hack)* Pr-prove it.

RED: *(Sigh)* Really... Okay I'll do it.

(RED picks up the biggest tree in the back yard.)

RED: *(Grunts)* See!

BLUE: Okay okay okay, put it down before you drop it and freaking smash my house!

(RED slowly puts the tree down.)

BLUE: Thank god! I thought you were gonna smash up my house!

RED: Oh nonononononono NO! I'll never do that, I live there now.

BLUE: Hold up hold up hold up! You live with who now!

RED: Hey look, we are partners and I live with you so just deal.

BLUE: What the—NO!

RED: I have to!

BLUE: Okay you! Can sleep in the shed in the backyard.

RED: That dirty old stinky thing.

BLUE: Monday through Thursday okay!

RED: Good! Friday we can be turned-up together!

BLUE: Um... No tomorrow I gotta go to GameStop and get Mario Kart 8, the new Super Smash Bros, Saints Row 4, GTA 5 and the Legend of Zelda Hyrule wo—

RED: Whatever I'mma DJ!

BLUE: What type?

RED: Well... Dubstep!

BLUE: No...

RED: Me and Skrillex are best pals!

BLUE: I hate dubstep I'm more of a gamer.

RED: Me too I'm a gamer, ex-boxer world champ, DJ, Brony and I'm in the World Wide Anime Club.

BLUE: Ex-world wide boxer champ?

RED: Oh yeah on my last fight I kicked the dude in the face an—

BLUE: Um never mind, I need some wood. And what was the UFO thing they said on the news: are you even human?

RED: Well duh I am a part of you, and the "UFO" wasn't flying, I was putting the crystal tree seed in the ground.

BLUE: Why do I need another tree back here, look at all these trees.

RED: This is not a normal tree! This tree is a crystal tree, it brings power to me and it gives you power so you can be strong like me! So we can fight evil but too much power can drive you insane but yeah... That's the... Oh and we gotta take care of it because evil is out here.

BLUE: So the tree is evil?

RED: *(Facepalm)* Just be careful. Oh and the new Flame Fox is always wrong, watch Red Hippo News instead.

BLUE: Okay...?

RED: Well I'm sleepy, I'm gonna go sleep in the shed.

(BLUE picks up wood and goes in the house.)

(The next day is a warm Friday morning. The nice smell of pancakes flows through the air. The best part is that there is no school.)

RED: Get up, come on we gotta go!

BLUE: (Waking up) Huh what. No you go back in your shed!

RED: We gotta check out some weapons!

BLUE: You mean you gotta go check out some weapons.

RED: Get up sleepy head! It's time for weapons and I made some pancakes.

BLUE: Pancakes! I'll be ready in an hour!

(Later.)

BLUE: Okay I'm ready.

RED: (Eating) Oh hey.

BLUE: You ATE everything!

RED: Oh... Anyway, come on!

BLUE: I don't have a car...

RED: Why.

BLUE: Well I did but—I let my friend drive but—um...

RED: Oh well we gotta walk.

(Later, at the weapon place.)

BLUE: Wait! SJ?!?

SJ: Blue?!

RED: You know her?

BLUE: Well duh her brother is—

KURO: Her brother is what!!

RED: You're her brother!?

KURO: Duh, anyway why are you here.

RED: He's the new member in the Domo Clan!

KURO: What!?!

RED: How do you know him?

SJ: He's in the same class that I'm in.

RED: Well anyway we need to get Blue a weapon...

SJ: Oh... Okay follow me.

(Presses button that leads to a wall that's covered in weapons.)

BLUE: Waaooh...

SJ: Choose a weapon. What do you sometimes fight with?

BLUE: Umm with my fists.

SJ: I know your weapon!

BLUE: That quick?

SJ: Well duh you're easy, you use iron fists, well ... gloves.

BLUE: That sounds too heavy.

SJ: Stop complaining and try it on!

(SJ puts the gloves on BLUE.)

BLUE: Gwahh!

SJ: Calm down and put all the weight on your feet, focus...

BLUE: Nnngg... I'm—I'm doing it!

SJ: Okay good, next try to walk.

BLUE: Ah-ahhh... I can't do that!

SJ: Shut it and try! Okay!

BLUE: Okay?...

(BLUE follows SJ's instructions.)

SJ: Follow me... Left... Right... Left right left right left right left...

BLUE: Raaaaaaaaaaaaaaaah!!!

SJ: You can do it!!

RED: Would you two hurry up!

SJ: Now punch! And ... kick!

BLUE: Hyee ah!

SJ: Alright shut up you're giving me a headache. Train more at home.

BLUE: Okay so what now?

SJ: You have your weapon, you know how to use it, what else... You leave duh.

BLUE: Alright! See you... (Leaves)

SJ: Wait!!! Make sure no one knows you came h— (Door closes)

(Later, walking to the store.)

RED: So how was your training.

BLUE: It hurt...

(Somewhere unknown.)

MINION 1: Sir... We've found him...

MINION 2: We've also found this. (Shows the gem)

???: Good but where are the others.

MINION 1: Others?

???: How dare you think a dark lord such as myself only has one gem!?! (Chokes MINION 1 to death.)

MINION 1: Ack uk... But sir... He... Has a— a— (Dies)

MINION 2: Oh Lord please don't be this way!

DARK LORD: Oh no I'm not gonna kill you... I have a job for you to do.

MINION 2: Yes Lord, what is it?

DARK LORD: I want you to find his stash and kill him and anyone else that gets in the way, bring some backup...
Now be gone, I have some work to do. *(Evil look)*

MINION 2: Ye— Yes sir!

To be continued...

Detention

by Finalist Zach Stone

Characters:
BRADLEY
MISS FORKE
RANDOM CLASSMATE IN DETENTION

BRADLEY: It started out like a normal day... I woke up, got ready and went to school and impatiently sat through all my incredibly boring classes. My name is Bradley Smith. I'm 13 years old, and I'm the best drawer in my school. Everything I draw is so realistic that sometimes people mistake my drawings for real things. One time I was doodling spiders on some notes in math class, and my friend sitting next to me jumped out of his skin when he saw it. Besides scaring people, my drawings also get me in trouble a lot. I do most of my drawings in class instead of taking notes. Today is the day my family is throwing my younger brother a surprise birthday and my parents are going to ground me for 3 months if I'm not home in time to yell "SURPRISE!" Today, I also have after school detention with the meanest and scariest teacher in my whole school, and possibly the world. Miss Forke. She's not the sharpest tool in the shed, but if you get on her bad side, it could ruin your whole life. Unfortunately, I am her bad side. Oh, and one more thing that I forgot to mention about myself, I have a magic pencil.

MISS FORKE: I have taught History for 60 years, 50 of those years have been here, at Utensil Middle School. I started out as a 6th grade teacher but I switched to 8th grade after my first year. The material wasn't hard or confusing, grading tests was fine. No, I switched for one reason and one reason only, I hate the little brats. During my first few years being a teacher, I taught at elementary schools and one day for show and tell, a little boy brought in his pet spider and it escaped from its cage. It was a highly poisonous spider and when the class found it, it was crawling up my arm and biting me. I started hallucinating and might have accidently dismissed the students halfway through the day. Long story short, I got fired, and got arachnophobia. But I have been working at this school longer than any of the other teachers and I've never, in my 60 years of teaching, met a boy so annoying and so obnoxious. That boy has the attention span of a fruit fly. One second he'll be taking notes and the next second he'll be drawing swords or fantasy creatures. I hope to one day finally put an end to his drawing days.

(BRADLEY walks into detention twenty seconds late, keeping his head down and trying not to make eye contact with MISS FORKE.)

MISS FORKE: Bradley Steven Smith...

BRADLEY: *(Aside)* Yeah, you heard her, she uses my middle name. It's super embarrassing and annoying.

MISS FORKE: ...You're late. Detention!

BRADLEY: But I already have detention.

MISS FORKE: Oh. Well, then you'll have to stay until 4:00 instead of 3:30.

BRADLEY: Could I come to make it up another day Miss Forke?

MISS FORKE: No!

BRADLEY: But Miss Forke, my family is throwing my brother a surprise birthday party and my parents are going to get super mad if I'm late and I have to be there to yell surprise at exactly 4:00.

MISS FORKE: Oh well then in that case, sure.

BRADLEY: Really?

MISS FORKE: No! You must be punished for not paying attention in class and then having the audacity to walk into detention late.

BRADLEY: But I was only twenty seconds late. And I wouldn't have been late if my locker hadn't been jammed and there was no one to help open it.

MISS FORKE: Your excuses are just going to get you into even more trouble so just sit down and get to work on homework and absolutely no drawings, that's what got you in here in the first place. Unless of course you'd like to write "I will take notes and pay attention in class instead of drawing foolish things" one hundred times.

BRADLEY: Okay, I'll do my homework... *(Aside)* ...for Art class. *(Stifles a laugh)*

MISS FORKE: Good. But don't let me see that drawing pencil out or I'll take it away until June and you'll be doing lines until June as well.

BRADLEY: Yes Miss Forke.

(BRADLEY trudges to the very back of the room and slouches down in a chair in a huff. He takes his binder out and from it his homework and his magic pencil.)

BRADLEY: *(Aside)* This pencil is somehow linked with my brain and it's magic because if I will it to do so, my drawings are transferred to real life. But, if I want to make the drawing disappear, all I do is tap the drawing with the pencil.

(BRADLEY draws a picture of Skittles. Then he pulls a mysterious bag of Skittles out of his pocket and starts to unhappily chew on his wonderful rainbow candy and tries to think of a way to escape detection and make it back to his house in time.)

MISS FORKE: Okay delinquents, it's 3:30, get out of here.

BRADLEY: *(Aside)* I'm going to try to sneak out in the pack of other people here. Miss Forke doesn't have her glasses on so I don't think she'll recognize me.

RANDOM CLASSMATE IN DETENTION: Hey Bradley, where are you going? Don't you have extra detention?

BRADLEY: Ah screw you John.

MISS FORKE: Bradley do you want to stay until 4:30?

BRADLEY: No.

MISS FORKE: THEN SIT DOWN!

BRADLEY: Yes Miss Forke. *(Walks back to the back of the room and sits down)*

BRADLEY: *(Aside)* I have to find some way to get out of here. *(Thinks for a second or two)* I've got it, I'll sneak away, and draw something that will distract her.

MISS FORKE: Come sit at the front of the room so I can keep a better eye on you. And stop talking to yourself, I'm trying to read my book.

BRADLEY: What book are you reading?

MISS FORKE: *(Looks down at her book)* It's called "How to cure Arachnophobia".

BRADLEY: *(Slowly and quietly picks up his backpack)* Why are you reading that?

MISS FORKE: I developed a very strong fear of spiders when I first started teaching.

BRADLEY: *(Aside)* That's it! I'll draw a spider. *(Bends over his desk so MISS FORKE doesn't see his paper)*

MISS FORKE: Ahhhhhhhhh! A spider.

BRADLEY: What? Where? *(He looks to where MISS FORKE is pointing.)*

MISS FORKE: Kill it. Kill it. Kill it. Kill it.

BRADLEY: If I kill it will you let me go home?

MISS FORKE: Never!

BRADLEY: Suit yourself.

MISS FORKE: Fine. Fine. Fine. If you can protect me from the spider, I'll let you go home.

BRADLEY: Deal.

(MISS FORKE gets up on her desk. BRADLEY runs over to the spider and bends down to tap it with the pencil that made it. Nothing happens.)

BRADLEY: Uh oh. It needs to be sharpened. *(Runs over to pencil sharpener)*

MISS FORKE: It's getting closer!

BRADLEY: Done! Die spider. *(Throws his pencil at the spider)*

MISS FORKE: Oh thank you so much. You may go. *(Jumps down off her desk and CRACK lands on the pencil)*

BRADLEY: Noooooooo. *(Runs out of the classroom)* Well at least I'll be able to make it home in time. *(Beat)* In the end, I made it back to my house at 3:59, but it turned out that I had remembered the time of my brother's surprise party an hour early. I thought it was four, but it was actually at five soooo yeah. I lost my awesome, amazing, magical pencil for nothing. But I had also learned a valuable lesson and will now pay attention in class. Another good thing was now I'm on Miss Forke's good side. Ever since I killed that spider she treats me like an angel.

End of Play

Why Not?

by Finalist Carlos Espinosa

Characters:
EMILIO VAQUEZ
MAYA VAQUEZ, Emilio's mom
MR. O
GABBY LUNA
DANNY WITTMEN, G.G.H.S. commentator
KAREN KELLY, G.G.H.S. commentator
COACH BARRY
STRANGE MAN/MR. WAJCIECHOWSKI

SCENE:
EMILIO: If only there was some easier way to get my grades up in Mr. O's Spanish class, man!! I MEAN HOW HARD IT CAN BE! I'M FREAKING SPANISH MYSELF! This would be a great time for my Dominican culture to KICK in! I think I'm doing the best I can in Spanish class, but I think that Mr. O just doesn't like me.

MAYA: Don't you have a championship game next Friday?

EMILIO: YES! Stop changing the subject but that's why I'm trying my hardest to get my grades up in Mr. O's class.

MAYA: Well, you gotta face this yourself, honey. I'm not always going to be there to fight your battles, *(Under her breath)* especially this one.

EMILIO: No Mom, I think I can handle it myself, but Mr. O knows I love basketball and I'm the school's star player for the Varsity team. I just don't know why he is being so unreasonable.

(The next day, EMILIO walks into class with GABBY.)

GABBY: Emilio, I'm trying to help you.

EMILIO: Gabby, you know I love you, but I can't take your help. I need to be a man and face Mr. O myself.

GABBY: Can I at least go with you after school to talk to him?

EMILIO: *(Laughing a little)* I know since you're my girlfriend you want to be there for me, but I can handle myself. Thank you anyway.

MR. O: *(Spanish accent)* Stop talking and sit in your seats right now! I'm tired of telling you guys to be quiet!

EMILIO: *(Looking puzzled)* Umm... Excuse me Mr. O...

MR. O: *(Sighing, a little mad)* Yes, Mr. Vaquez. What is it now!?

EMILIO: Can I talk to you after school?

MR. O: I'll think about it later, but we need to start class so shushhhh!

(After class. Everyone leaves the class while EMILIO waits in his seat.)

EMILIO: Mr. O, whatever happened to us.

MR. O: *(Disgusted look)* Ewww, Emilio don't be disgusting!

EMILIO: No! Mr. O not like that. Jeez. I was talking about our student-teacher relationship. We were cool since 9th grade till now. I'm a freaking 12th grader about to go to college. Do you know how many offers I got so far? I got four from great colleges that I wouldn't mind going to. I got offers to Duke, University of Maryland, Providence College and Kentucky. But the only thing holding me back is you, Mr. O. Why?

MR. O: I want you to know that I like all my students equally, but my reason why I don't like you as much is...

(GABBY quickly opens the door yelling at him.)

GABBY: Mr. O, Emilio is a good student, and you just don't want him to succeed in life. That's why you give him such a hard time! You treat Emilio SO! different 'cause you're jealous. You just wanted to be just like him when you were young DIDN'T! you MR. O!

MR. O: *(Very angry)* WHO THE HELL DO YOU THINK YOU ARE COMING IN HERE TELLING ME WHAT I BEEN THROUGH!!! See, all you kids assume you know everything. Ms. Luna, if you don't get out of my DAMN classroom in 10 seconds, I'll make sure you don't attend graduation! 1... 2... 3... 4... 5... 6... 7!!!

GABBY: Okay okay! I'm gone.

(EMILIO runs to the door and screams.)

EMILIO: What kind of help was that?!?!?!?!?

(MR. O takes a seat with a big sigh.)

MR. O: *(Holding his head)* Ahh kids nowadays... *(Small chuckle)*

EMILIO: *(Agreeing)* Tell me about it...

MR. O: *(Laughing)* Shut up.

EMILIO: So you gonna tell me why, Mr. O?

MR. O: Ohh, yeah sure. I was gonna say that I was just like you when I was young. I was a star soccer player, had the best-looking girl in school, and I was great in Spanish. Life couldn't be any sweeter, right? *(MR. O smiles.)*

EMILIO: Right?

MR. O: *(Serious)* Wrong! See Emilio, I am your uncle, but the reason I don't like you is because of your mother.

EMILIO: *(Surprised)* MY MOTHER!! What does she have to do with anything!?!?!?

146

MR. O: My sister who is your mother is family. We grew apart when we were young. This was because of our parents. They didn't want us meeting each other. My father was mad at my mother and my mother was mad at my father. He told us lies about each other. Mom hated Dad and Dad hated Mom, they never could agree on anything they wanted. Dad said I was the better child and Mom told Maya that she was the better child. It was just an ongoing thing.

EMILIO: Granma and Pa.

MR. O: Yes, they got divorced when I was 15 and she was 13. Your mom loved her parents both, but she had to pick one to live with for the rest of her young life. I went with my dad, your grandpa, and we both went our separate ways. We were never really mad at each other, we were just mad at our parents for separating us. Our parents always used to argue.

EMILIO: Yehh I get that you had family problems, but why were you mad at me.

MR. O: Because you came from my sister! No I'm just kidding. *(Laughing)* But I'm proud that she raised a young man like you. But I'm hard on you because, YOU'RE A FREAKING SENIOR. You need pressure. Nothing you get is easy unless it is given to you.

EMILIO: Well that's good to know, but why weren't you mean to me my 9th, 10th and 11th grade years?

MR. O: Because I wanted you to get comfortable in my classroom. I wanted to convince you that I was your friend.

EMILIO: Yehh and it worked! But one more question.

MR. O: Yes.

EMILIO: Am I really failing your class?

MR. O: *(Chuckling)* Ohh no Emilio, believe it or not you have an A- in my class. I was just so mad that I wanted you to feel like you were failing my class, but you really had a good grade all along.

EMILIO: *(Puzzled)* Whaa?

MR. O: Yes just think of it as a big serious joke. *(Laughing)* Now we can talk later, go to practice and get your work done and I'll see you tomorrow and maybe even game day. *(Winks at EMILIO in a friendly way)*

EMILIO: *(Smiles)* Okay Mr. O, I'll see you tomorrow. *(Rushing out the door)* I won't let you down Mr. O. *(Gives MR. O a thumbs-up)*

(Game day.)

DANNY: Danny Wittmen here reporting live with Karen Kelly from the Gordon Grey High School Gymnasium, and I'll tell you folks it is livelier than a Bruno Mars concert in this gymnasium.

KAREN: Tell me about it, Danny, we have two very athletic and physical teams right here. We have the Pam Pucket Grizzles going up against our mighty Gordon Grey Wolves.

DANNY: Mighty indeed, Karen. It looks like this game will probably come down to the last shot.

KAREN KELLY: If in the right hands, Danny.

DANNY WITTMEN: You got that right, Karen.

GABBY: Emilio! Heyy.

EMILIO: Gabby hey.

GABBY: I just wanted to wish you good luck on your game, and whatever happens just remember that you tried your best to get this far.

(STRANGE MAN with a clipboard bumps EMILIO.)

STRANGE MAN: Excuse me.

EMILIO: Jeez dude watch where you're going.

GABBY: Yehh jerk!

(STRANGE MAN walks to the bleachers with the other fans and sits and writes on his clipboard.)

EMILIO: (Laughing) Yehh uhh, thanks Gabby. I'll need it.

GABBY: Okay, I'll leave you to warm up. I got to go cheerlead, so bye. (Smiling, gives EMILIO a hug.)

EMILIO: Alright love you babe, bye.

(GABBY blows a kiss to EMILIO. EMILIO stretches while GABBY walks away.)

KAREN: Karen Kelly here with Danny Wittmen. Welcome back to some great high school basketball. The Grey Wolves' top scorer Emilio Vaquez with 41 points, 11 assists, 2 blocks and 13 rebounds.

DANNY: Yes Karen he is all over the place. The score is 73-73 with 3.4 seconds on the clock. The teams break from their huddles. Now Karen, if they make this shot they win. If they miss it they will have to go into overtime. The Wolves can't have that happen, they don't have any big men that are NOT in foul trouble. They got to rely on this last shot, which is a 99% chance that he might miss this.

KAREN: You got that right, I got my fingers crossed.

DANNY: Arron Beck inbounds the ball, Emilio Vaquez catches it. Emilio shoots. 3. 2. 1. Buzzer sounds. Emilio hits the floor. AND IT'S IN!!!! OFF THE GLASS! EMILIO VAQUEZ WINS IT FOR THE GREY WOLVES!!!

KAREN: Danny this isn't good, Emilio isn't getting up. I think he is injured.

DANNY: Yes, he looks very hurt and he grabbing his left ankle. It's swollen purple.

COACH BARRY: Emilio are you okay? Tell me what's hurting.

EMILIO: (In pain on the floor) It's my ankle.

148

COACH BARRY: It looks bad, let's get him to hospital.

EMILIO: Ughh my head hurts. *(EMILIO covers his eyes and passes out.)*

COACH BARRY: Let's get you to a hospital.

(EMILIO wakes up in the hospital and sees MAYA and MR. O talking.)

EMILIO: *(Looking woozy)* Ughhh what happened.

GABBY: *(Sitting next to his hospital bed)* I'll tell you what happened, you broke your ankle and got a mild concussion.

EMILIO: That explains why I can't see very good now, but how did this happen? And did we win the game? Where is everybody?

GABBY: Calm down Emilio. *(Laughing)* We did win and it was all because of you for hitting that buzzer beater in the last 3 seconds. But when that defender was defending you he elbowed you in the head while he was in the air and landed on your ankle, and, you know, broke it.

EMILIO: Ohhh okay, so we're champions?

GABBY: Yehh we are dummy, *(Smiling)* all because of you.

(STRANGE MAN knocks on door. MR. O opens the door and shakes hands with him.)

MR. O: Hey you must be Mr. Wojciechowski. How are you?

MR. WOJCIECHOWSKI: I'm fine, the bigger question is how is our "superstar" doing over there.

(MR. WOJCIECHOWSKI shakes EMILIO's hand.)

EMILIO: Hey haven't I seen you before?

GABBY: *(Sassy)* Yehh that's the jerk who bumped you, remember?

EMILIO: Chill out Gabby.

MR. WOJCIECHOWSKI: Yes I was that "jerk" I believe.

GABBY: *(Feeling sorry a little)* Ohh yehh, well, sorry about that.

MR. WOJCIECHOWSKI: *(Chuckling a little)* No problem.

EMILIO: So what brings you over here?

MR. WOJCIECHOWSKI: Well I don't know if you know me or not, but I'm Steve Wojciechowski, the head basketball coach of Marquette University. I'm here to offer you a full paid basketball scholarship to Marquette University. After displaying your basketball skills like that, you deserve this opportunity!

EMILIO: *(Super surprised)* Are you serious?!?!?!?!?

MR. WOJCIECHOWSKI: Definitely!

EMILIO: Yes I'll take it, thank you so much!!

MR. WAJCIECHOWSKI: As soon as you're up and out of this hospital call me, we'll keep in touch. And by the way don't thank me, thank your teacher, Mr. O.

EMILIO: Mr. O?

MAYA: Yes, Mr. O. *(She hugs him.)*

GABBY: Ms. Vaquez!! Aren't you married?! I'm telling Mr. Vaquez!

MAYA: *(Giggling)* Yes I am, but I'm just showing some love to my brother that I haven't seen in forever.

MR. O: This is true. Gabby, I'm Maya's older brother.

(GABBY looks at EMILIO.)

EMILIO: Yehh it's true. But did you guys make up?

MR. O: Yes! We did and we caught up on old times, too.

MAYA: *(Laughing)* Yehh we did.

EMILIO: That's great! I'm happy for both of you. I just wanted to say thank you Uncle O. You planned it all out perfectly.

GABBY: Yehh you did Mr. O.

MR. O: I know Marquette is the perfect fit for you. Their basketball team is great and with the help of you it could be even better, and it's not far from Gabby's university either so you guys could still see each other.

EMILIO: I don't know what to say Uncle O. Thank you. I couldn't have done it without you.

MR. O: Heyy, *(Laughing)* why not.

End of Play

Back Bone

by Finalist Toniesha Johnson

Characters:
SHACKAH
SAMANTHA
KHALIL
OFFICER

SCENE: _Lies and deceit plague Shackah, a young girl who's head over heels in love. Unfortunately, the love of her life is in love with someone else. That someone else is Shackah's best friend Samantha, one of the most conniving, deceitful, and spiteful young ladies that you will ever come in contact with in your life. The story starts with SHACKAH and SAMANTHA outside KHALIL's house._

(SHACKAH hands SAMANTHA her cell phone with anger.)

SHACKAH: Do you know why Khalil didn't show up to our parenting class last night?

SAMANTHA: No... _(With a puzzled look on her face)_ Why did you ask me that?

SHACKAH: I called him a thousand times last night and no answer, but yet you seem to reach him just fine.

SAMANTHA: What are you talking about?

SHACKAH: _(In a loud tone)_ Bitch you have two answered calls from him, how come you didn't say you heard from him? Here I am crying, and you're just sitting there.

(SAMANTHA walks away, rolling her eyes and smacking her teeth.)

SAMANTHA: Girl bye...

(KHALIL emerges from the house.)

KHALIL: Hey baby.

(KHALIL walks up to SHACKAH and leans in for a kiss. SHACKAH turns her head.)

SAMANTHA: You are looking at this the wrong way.

SHACKAH: Whatever.

(SHACKAH walks away with anger. As KHALIL begins to follow SHACKAH, SAMANTHA grabs him by the arm and pulls him back.)

KHALIL: What are you doing, do you want her to find out about us.

SAMANTHA: _(With a loud tone)_ YES!

(KHALIL holds, kisses and caresses SAMANTHA.)

KHALIL: Why can't we just run away together, let's forget about her. She can have the baby; I'll pay child support, I'll do it all, I just want to be with you.

SAMANTHA: She can't have your baby, she will never make a good mom, not like I can... I told you a week ago to get rid of her.

(KHALIL lets her go and turns his back.)

KHALIL: But what about the baby, my son.

(SAMANTHA gently kisses him on the lips.)

SAMANTHA: She can never have your child, if that baby lives then she will always be. Don't worry I have a plan.

(SAMANTHA whispers something in KHALIL's ear. KHALIL pulls away shocked and confused.)

KHALIL: WHAT! Have you lost your mind, she's a human being.

SAMANTHA: And she is a waste of space and she will be dealt with.

(SAMANTHA grabs KHALIL close.)

SAMANTHA: I will get rid of her tonight, and tomorrow will be a new beginning. I promise we can be together forever.

(They both walk out of sight.)

(Later on that day the threesome find themselves in SAMANTHA's living room with no one home. They are all on the couch, SHACKAH lays in KHALIL's arms on the love seat, while SAMANTHA sits alone on the La-Z-Boy with hatred in her written all over her face... Soon she and KHALIL catch eyes and SAMANTHA nods her head as if to signal KHALIL. They both look at SHACKAH and to their surprise she is fast asleep in KHALIL's arms. She looks so peaceful, so happy.)

(SAMANTHA gets off the couch and ushers KHALIL to move from under SHACKAH, then she grabs the couch cushion, places it over her head and pushes.)

SHACKAH: (Muffled) Get off me.

SAMANTHA: Just die.

(KHALIL watches in horror as SAMANTHA smothers SHACKAH with no remorse until her body falls limp and cold.)

KHALIL: (Falling to his knees while SAMANTHA rejoices) You killed her.

SAMANTHA: I know, and now we can be together.

KHALIL: I can't.

SAMANTHA: What do you mean you can't?

KHALIL: I can't do this; I can't walk around with this weight on my shoulders.

SAMANTHA: You can, and you will.

(SAMANTHA hands KHALIL the pillow she used to smother SHACKAH with, he grabs it and cries on it. SAMANTHA walks up to his weeping body.)

SAMANTHA: *(In a low monotone)* By the way, your fingerprints are all over the murder weapon so if you wuss out, you're dead meat, then it's your words against mine.

(As she talks, KHALIL's face fills with shock. Suddenly it freezes and becomes stuck as if he detached himself from the reality of the situation.)

SAMANTHA: Get your punk ass up and help me hide the body.

KHALIL: No.

(SAMANTHA looks at KHALIL as if he is speaking Spanish.)

SAMANTHA: No... You mean yes.

(KHALIL stands up and speaks loudly.)

KHALIL: You go to hell you selfish piece of shit.

(SAMANTHA smacks KHALIL across his face.)

SAMANTHA: You son of a bitch.

(KHALIL grabs his camera phone. As SAMANTHA turns and grabs SHACKAH's body he snaps a picture.)

SAMANTHA: What was that?

(KHALIL runs out the door as fast as he can—he never looks back. He keeps running until he sees a police OFFICER sitting at the liquor store.)

KHALIL: Officer, I just watched my girlfriend get murdered by her best friend.

(The OFFICER jumps out of his car.)

OFFICER: Stop, breathe, what is your name young man?

KHALIL: Man forget my name, I need you to get this psycho.

(KHALIL pulls out his phone and reveals the picture to the OFFICER.)

OFFICER: I know her. That's Sammy, where is she?

KHALIL: She's four blocks down at her house.

(The OFFICER makes the call through his walkie-talkie.)

(The scene fades to the OFFICER and his colleagues assessing the crime scene and hauling SAMANTHA into the back of the cop car. KHALIL stands there staring into space not able to comprehend the situation.)

OFFICER: You did the right thing, it takes courage and back bone to do what you did.

KHALIL: I didn't love her but I loved my unborn son enough to know that this just wasn't right. Now I have nothing.

OFFICER: Yes you do have something; you have the one thing most people lack.

KHALIL: Yea and what's that?

OFFICER: Character, you should be proud of yourself. I'm sorry for your loss.

KHALIL: Me too.

(The OFFICER gets into the driver seat of his car and pulls away. SAMANTHA watches KHALIL, gazing angrily into his eyes until she is no longer in view, never to be seen again.)

End of Play

The Hero Who Called Himself Faith

by Finalist Scott Lake

Characters:
JAMES, the hero and main character
MOM
DAD
FREDRIC, helper and companion to James. One of the three sons.
DRAGON
FRANCIS, old guy who lives on top of the Thousand Steps of Pain. One of the three sons.
DEMON TROOP 1
DEMON TROOP 2
DEMON KING
DEMON ADVISOR
NICHOLAS, old man. One of the three sons.

SCENE 1: _Our story takes place in the west, in a small village. In that village is a child who loves to explore and do hard puzzles and joke around. This child's name is James and it is his 14th birthday. His parents told him when he was 14 he could go on adventures out of the village. When JAMES is going home he sees his DAD outside waiting near the door. JAMES goes inside and sees that his MOM and DAD have a cake waiting for him._

JAMES: Today is my 14th birthday and now I can go on my journey to look for the three legendary weapons and defeat the Demon King. Before I go on my journey I should go home first so I can say goodbye to my mom and dad. Mom, Dad, are you home?

MOM and DAD: Yes James.

JAMES: Hello Mom, hello Dad, I'm going on my journey.

DAD: Before you go on your journey, James, you must have a companion. Luckily we found someone who can come with you.

MOM: Come in.

(Door opening sound.)

FREDRIC: Hi James my name is Fredric.

JAMES: I do not trust you.

FREDRIC: I will explain why I was picked to help you for this journey, but not here. There are spies of the Demon King here so we must go now—grab your stuff that you will need then we shall go.

JAMES: OK, I would like to hear you explain how I can trust you.

FREDRIC: OK see you in a few minutes.

(Outside on a road walking to the mountains.)

FREDRIC: Now I can explain. We can set up camp here—now here is my story. My father was the first man who made three legendary weapons and defeated the Demon King.

JAMES: Really? Where is your proof? It is hard to believe that.

FREDRIC: OK here is my proof.

(FREDRIC pulls out a tiny box that has a small silver object.)

FREDRIC: This is a piece of the Sword of Faith, when you hold this it will tell you where the Sword of Faith is.

JAMES: OK.

(JAMES picks up the small silver object.)

JAMES: I see a cave in the mountains now and it seems not so far, and I see the sword too.

FREDRIC: Now do you believe me?

JAMES: Yes I believe you, Fredric, but why could you not go to it?

FREDRIC: Because only you could see it and get it, because you were chosen for this. We will start heading there tomorrow, you will need your rest.

SCENE 2:

(They are on the mountains near the entrance of the cave.)

JAMES: We are here.

FREDRIC: Wait before you go down there.

JAMES: Why?

FREDRIC: Something is wrong, someone is here.

JAMES: Who?

FREDRIC: It looks like some demon troops are here.

JAMES: How do you know that?

FREDRIC: Look down, I see them.

JAMES: Now I see them. Do they know that the Sword of Faith is in there?

FREDRIC: I guess, so they must be trying to get the Sword of Faith. This might be a problem.

JAMES: Could they get the Sword of Faith?

FREDRIC: Trust me, my father would put a guardian to protect the Sword of Faith.

JAMES: What kind of guardian?

(Then there is a very loud roar that comes out of the cave.)

FREDRIC: A dragon.

JAMES: What? Why does it have to be a dragon!

FREDRIC: There was a dragon that was loyal to my father.

JAMES: So how do I get the Sword of Faith without dying?

FREDRIC: You have to figure that out on your own.

JAMES: So you can't come with me.

FREDRIC: Yes, have fun. I have faith in you James.

JAMES: Thanks, next time you see me I will have the Sword of Faith.

(JAMES enters the cave: it smells really bad and there is a door with words around it.)

JAMES: The cave smells like dead crops. Why are there so many swords on the ground? I should grab one, it might come in handy. The dragon must be behind that door.

(JAMES walks to the door and realizes that there are words on the door.)

JAMES: What is this: "I shall only raise my sword to Evil and put it down for Good." So how does that help me beat the dragon? This is crazy, I can't beat a dragon. But is he Evil.

(When JAMES opens the door it makes a rusty sound and then there is a huge roar followed by a huge burst of fire coming right at JAMES. JAMES dodges it before it hits him. Then another burst of fire comes at him. JAMES dodges it again.)

JAMES: Wait why am I fighting this? The dragon is not evil, it's just doing its job. So if I put down my sword...

(JAMES stabs his sword in the ground. Then another burst of fire comes at him—just before it hits him it stops. JAMES opens his eyes.)

JAMES: I'm not dead.

DRAGON: Interesting.

JAMES: Who said that?

DRAGON: I did.

(Then another burst of fire comes but it is not at JAMES, it is at the wall. It lights up the wall making the cave brighter.)

DRAGON: You are the first person who solved the riddle.

JAMES: Wait, you can talk?

DRAGON: Yes, you can talk too, so how is this surprising?

JAMES: It is not every day when a dragon talks.

DRAGON: Good point, here is your prize.

(The DRAGON grabs a case and pulls out the Sword of Faith.)

DRAGON: What is your name?

JAMES: James.

DRAGON: James I award you the Sword of Faith, take your prize.

(When JAMES holds the sword it starts to glow.)

DRAGON: You are the next person. There will be people who will stop from your goal and there will be people who will help you too. Now I can leave.

JAMES: Why?

DRAGON: I am finished with my duty. We will meet again James, one day.

(Then DRAGON flies out of the cave. JAMES leaves the cave with the Sword of Faith in hand.)

JAMES: I got it Fredric.

FREDRIC: I see.

JAMES: Now what?

FREDRIC: Onward to the next place now. We are going to my brother's house to get the Helm of Wisdom, it is somewhere in the south.

(Near the cliffs looking at the JAMES and the Sword.)

DEMON TROOP 1: We must tell our king about this. He will not be happy about this, so you tell him.

DEMON TROOP 2: OK.

(In the far north where even the grass will not grow and sun will not shine, a very dark kingdom lays there.)

DEMON TROOP 2: Sire we bring you news about the Sword of Faith.

(A very inhuman voice.)

DEMON KING: Yes what is it, did you get the sword?

DEMON TROOP 2: No.

DEMON KING: What is it then?

DEMON TROOP 2: Someone got it before we did.

DEMON KING: What!

(Then the DEMON KING throws his sword at the DEMON TROOPS.)

DEMON TROOP 2: Uuuuuuuuuuuuuuuuu.

DEMON KING: Loyal advisor, come here.

DEMON ADVISOR: Yes.

DEMON KING: Send troops to kill the child, but not too many troops, and make sure that this does not go out anywhere. It might make people have hope again, I do not want that.

DEMON ADVISOR: I will make the arrangements.

SCENE 3:

(Now back to JAMES and FREDRIC, the setting is in a forest hiding in a bush.)

FREDRIC: We better be careful because the Demon King knows you have the Sword of Faith.

JAMES: Good point, we should avoid villages. Are we close to our destination?

FREDRIC: Yes.

JAMES: What is it called?

FREDRIC: The Thousand Steps of Pain.

JAMES: Why is it called that?

FREDRIC: Because you have to walk up a thousand steps of pain.

JAMES: Great, more walking up steps now.

FREDRIC: Yes.

(JAMES and FREDRIC walk up the Steps of Pain panting and sweaty.)

JAMES: What step are we on?

FREDRIC: I think we have about 20 more to go.

JAMES: You said that at the last 100 steps.

FREDRIC: I see the top.

JAMES: Really?

FREDRIC: Yes.

JAMES: Hope there is water up there.

FREDRIC: Me too.

(They reach the top of the steps. There is a big house with huge doors, and the door is slowly opening. Out comes a man to greet JAMES and FREDRIC.)

MAN WHO CAME OUT OF THE HOUSE: Fredric is that you?

FREDRIC: Yes, can we have some water and come in?

MAN: Is this the kid that our father saw?

FREDRIC: Yes he is the kid.

MAN: What is your name kid?

JAMES: James, what is yours?

FRANCIS: I forgot to introduce myself. My name is Francis, keeper of the Helm of Wisdom. Nice to meet you. Do you have the Sword of Faith?

JAMES: Yes.

FRANCIS: Can I see it?

(JAMES unsheathes the Sword of Faith and shows it to FRANCIS.)

FRANCIS: It's beautiful. It's been a long time.

JAMES: So can I have the Helm of Wisdom?

FRANCIS: Uuuuuuuuuuuuuuuu no.

JAMES: Why not.

FRANCIS: What is the fun in that? If I just gave it to you without earning it there would be no point. You have to work for it. I have to train you—it will be fun.

JAMES: Let's start training.

FRANCIS: No.

JAMES: Why not?

FRANCIS: You need your sleep, trust me. See you tomorrow.

(It is tomorrow, it is very sunny and it is hot.)

JAMES: So what is your test.

FRANCIS: A sword fight, take me down.

JAMES: OK.

(JAMES charges at FRANCIS with his sword—next thing JAMES is face first on the ground.)

JAMES: Ow, that hurt.

FRANCIS: You can't just run at me like that again.

(JAMES looks at FRANCIS, trying to find a weak spot. FRANCIS charges at him. JAMES looks, then the sun gets in his eye and again JAMES is on the ground face-first.)

JAMES: Ow, the sun got in my eye.

FRANCIS: I used my surroundings.

(JAMES runs at FRANCIS but stops and throws dirt in FRANCIS's face. JAMES pushes him on the ground.)

FRANCIS: Good job.

JAMES: Do I get the helm?

FRANCIS: Yes.

JAMES: Really?

FRANCIS: No. You may have strength and power but there is one thing you do not have.

JAMES: What is that?

FRANCIS: You do not have the knowledge.

JAMES: What knowledge?

FRANCIS: Strategy. Yes, throwing dirt on my face was a good plan, but you can't always rely on that. Follow me.

(FRANCIS trains JAMES in sword play and some new moves.)

FRANCIS: I just lost to a kid.

JAMES: That was a good game but I still won.

(JAMES starts dancing. FRANCIS walks into a closet and pulls out the Helm of Wisdom.)

FRANCIS: I award you the Helm of Wisdom, use it wisely.

(Then FREDRIC opens the door with sweat on his face.)

FREDRIC: Demon troops are coming, I do not know how many.

JAMES: I do, he has ten.

FREDRIC: What, how do you know that?

JAMES: The Demon King would not send a whole army to kill me. It might be because he does not want the people to know about me.

FREDRIC: OK so what we should do?

JAMES: Wait for them.

FREDRIC: Why?

JAMES: I will defeat them on my own.

FREDRIC: No, I will help you.

(FRANCIS puts his arm on FREDRIC.)

FRANCIS: Let him do it, OK.

(JAMES opens the door and leaves.)

FREDRIC: You are crazy, he is not ready.

FRANCIS: Yes he is, I would bet on it.

FREDRIC: How much?

(FREDRIC and FRANCIS look at each other with a smile. FRANCIS and FREDRIC dig deep in their pockets and put their bets on the table.)

(JAMES looks at the sun then at the ground then sits down and waits.)

(The DEMON TROOPS are out of breath and sweaty.)

DEMON TROOP: There he is, kill him.

(JAMES attacks them. Two are blinded by the sun and defeated. Then JAMES throws dirt at them and three are defeated. The rest die because they are too tired to fight.)

(Then FRANCIS and FREDRIC come out of the house. FRANCIS stuffs some money in his pocket with a smile.)

FREDRIC: I am proud of you.

JAMES: One more thing to go, the Shield of Strength. Goodbye, Francis.

FRANCIS: Bye James. Hope you come back, I want a rematch.

(Back to the DEMON KING.)

DEMON KING: What is the report?

DEMON ADVISOR: He has the Helm of Wisdom.

DEMON KING: Get the army ready, he will come so I want all the troops from all the land here.

DEMON ADVISOR: I will make the arrangements. But what about the people, would that give them hope? They will know about him.

DEMON KING: Yes they will, but when all that happens, hope will die when I take his head as my trophy. There will never be a person in the world who will have hope again hahahahahahah.

SCENE 4:

(Back to JAMES and FREDRIC, they have entered a castle with many people staring at them.)

PERSON: Is that him, our hero who would defeat the Demon King and free us?

(JAMES and FREDRIC keep walking through the castle until they reach a stone courtyard. In the middle is an old fit man.)

NICHOLAS: James is the hero, right?

FREDRIC: Yes he is Nicholas.

NICHOLAS: Good. James, come here.

JAMES: What is your test?

NICHOLAS: *(With a sad face with no hope in his eyes)* I do not need to give you a test.

JAMES: Why?

NICHOLAS: You have already proven yourself to me. The next part you need the most strength for.

JAMES: What is that?

(NICHOLAS opens a door to show a crowd of troops; they look sad and without hope.)

NICHOLAS: Getting your troops to fight well for you is the test. Do not fail me, I have lost my strength.

(NICHOLAS gives JAMES a golden shield that is glowing.)

NICHOLAS: I give you the Shield of Strength, now lead us to victory.

(JAMES walks out of the courtyard and sees 10,000 knights looking at him.)

NICHOLAS: *(With a smile)* He is full once more.

(JAMES speaks in a loud voice like he is not a kid anymore.)

JAMES: We are men who have lived in fear all our lives, but now we have hope. If we go down in history it will be for our bravery. Will you fight with me or live in fear?

(There is stunned silence, then one knight stomps his feet, then more stomp theirs, then more and more until every knight stomps his feet.)

(JAMES leaves the crowd and walks back to NICHOLAS and FREDRIC.)

NICHOLAS: That was your real test and you have passed. I will be joining in the fight too.

FREDRIC: You are too old, you can't fight Nicholas.

NICHOLAS: If I can lift up a sword I can fight.

FREDRIC: I will fight too.

JAMES: The next battle ahead will be the hardest. Let's make a plan.

(They are at the kingdom of the DEMON KING, there are sounds of metal hitting metal. JAMES, FREDRIC and NICHOLAS are outside of throne room of the DEMON KING.)

JAMES: Beyond this point you cannot come.

FREDRIC and NICHOLAS: We know.

NICHOLAS: We will guard the door for you.

(JAMES opens the door and walks in.)

DEMON KING: You are weak, you have led your men to death.

(JAMES and the DEMON KING fight. The DEMON KING pushes JAMES back to a ledge.)

DEMON KING: You will fall as many other men will fall.

(The DEMON KING kicks JAMES off the ledge. JAMES starts to fall.)

JAMES: Is that how I die, falling? It can't be.

(JAMES closes his eyes then hits something hard. He hears the beating of wings.)

JAMES: Am I dead?

DRAGON: No.

(JAMES opens his eyes.)

JAMES: Where am I?

DRAGON: I think on my back.

JAMES: It's you.

DRAGON: I told you you would see me again.

JAMES: He is too strong, what should I do?

DRAGON: It's simple.

JAMES: What is it?

DRAGON: What does he fear?

JAMES: Me.

DRAGON: Are you ready?

JAMES: Yes.

(The DRAGON carries JAMES back to the DEMON KING.)

DEMON KING: You came back? You should have just fallen to your death, now your death will be more painful mmhahahaha.

JAMES: This time you will fall.

DEMON KING: How would I die? As long there is fear I will never die.

(JAMES jumps off the DRAGON right at the DEMON KING. DEMON KING raises his sword to stop his attack, the demon sword start to crack.)

DEMON KING: How can you beat me? There will always be fear, it is impossible to kill me.

JAMES: You are not fear, you just feed on it. Yes there will be fear, but not a feeder.

(The DEMON KING's sword cracks more.)

DEMON KING: Impossible.

JAMES: I have the hopes and dreams of people. As long there is that you will never come back.

(The DEMON KING's sword breaks.)

JAMES: Farewell, Demon.

DEMON KING: Noooooooooooooooooo...

(The sounds of metal hitting metal stop, then there is cheering.)

End of Play

Somebody to Love

by Finalist Donnice Robinson

Characters:
PRECIOUS
MOTHER, Precious' mother
AMELIN, Precious' friend
DEAN GOLDSMITH
CARL

SCENE 1: Opening.

PRECIOUS: Waking up in the morning with a stomachache every morning isn't the best feeling, but when you have little money and no food, the corner store with dollar chips and drinks is the only thing you can afford when you're searching your house for coins. My dad stepped out on me and my mom when I was 16, he moved away to live with his new family. My dad cheated on my mom and their 15 years marriage. My mom was thinking they just needed a break but when my dad took the option, he went out and got a lady pregnant. That's when I knew there was no coming back. Before my dad left our family was everything it was a smooth straight line. But now my mom and I don't get along, we barely talk ever. My dad broke our happy household to a sad depressing miserable hole. Also my mom doesn't care about anything, all she does is sleep, when mom first found out about dad and his little family she broke down completely. There's no getting her back. Although we don't have the right equipment to be healthy, or get to school, we have always had nice material things.

(Walking from her room to the bathroom with her hot pink rhinestone toothbrush in her right hand, PRECIOUS trips over a big bag of dirty laundry that's been sitting for some weeks. Her stomach begins to hurt as if there were two giant balls dancing against each other.)

MOTHER: Precious get up and stop acting crazy.

(MOTHER walks away to enter her room.)

PRECIOUS: *(Under her breath)* Why do you care?

SCENE 2:

AMELIN: Hey stranger where have you been? I almost forgot you were human. Were you hiding in a ditch or something?

PRECIOUS: Hahaha that's so funny, I almost forgot how corny you are.

AMELIN: No but seriously where have you been. I've been checking your classes and your progress. And as a friend I'm going to tell you this because I love you. YOUR GRADES SUCK!

PRECIOUS: Seriously why do you care?

AMELIN: Precious you're like the sister I've never had. I care for you girl, we have to get your grades up and fast.

PRECIOUS: And you're like the sister I never had BUT you care too much. I'm not saying don't care, just care less.

AMELIN: I love you Precious but sometimes, I wonder where your brain be at and if it's in your head, why don't you use it?

PRECIOUS: I would love to stay and talk about my brain BUT I have to go to class. See you.

AMELIN: Make sure you do work.

SCENE 3:

(Bell rings and class is now over. PRECIOUS and AMELIN are walking down the hall on their way to lunch.)

AMELIN: It's either I'm tripping or he was so checking you out.

PRECIOUS: Amelin please he's like the school hottie. Everybody wants to date him. Plus I don't have time for it. They really don't want anything but your goodies and give headaches.

AMELIN: Precious you have to stop. All guys isn't like your dad.

PRECIOUS: Whatever, you wouldn't understand.

(PRECIOUS walks off leaving AMELIN standing there.)

SCENE 4:

(PRECIOUS walks in her house from school with headphones in her ears, dancing to the beat of the song she's listening to. The phone rings.)

PRECIOUS: Hello?

MOTHER: I'll be home in about 15 minutes, I'll call you when I'm outside to help with the groceries.

PRECIOUS: GROCERIES? When you start buying groceries?

(PRECIOUS hangs up the phone with much attitude.)

SCENE 5:

MOTHER: Precious? PRECIOUS!

PRECIOUS: WHAT? WHAT? WHAT? Why are you yelling my name like a crazy person?

MOTHER: What did you just say to me little girl? If I haven't forgotten I'm your mother...

(Before MOTHER can finish, PRECIOUS rudely begins to talk over her.)

PRECIOUS: Save it. You don't care for me or how I feel, all you care about is you and your bed.

(MOTHER slaps her across her face. PRECIOUS looks up at her mother, tears fill her eyes.)

PRECIOUS: I HATE YOU. And your lazy ways.

(PRECIOUS then walks towards the door and leaves.)

SCENE 6:

(Two weeks later. PRECIOUS is rushing out of the house to get to school. Just when she steps in school the bell rings, which now means she is late for class.)

DEAN GOLDSMITH: By the looks of your attendance you have been here almost every day.

PRECIOUS: Yes!

DEAN GOLDSMITH: I'm proud of you, keep it up.

(PRECIOUS gives DEAN GOLDSMITH a slight smile, trying not to show how irritated she is.)

SCENE 7:

(CARL stops what he's doing to look at PRECIOUS take a seat in her seat in the class.)

PRECIOUS: We have a problem?

(CARL looks at her with a smile then walks away. The bell rings for school to be over.)

SCENE 8:

(PRECIOUS is now on her way to the bus stop to go home.)

CARL: Hey you need a ride?

PRECIOUS: I'm okay, my bus should be here in about 15 minutes.

CARL: Well, can I talk to you for them 15 minutes?

PRECIOUS: You can talk but there's a 0% chance that I'll be listening.

CARL: Is it that serious?

PRECIOUS: What serious?

CARL: I'm so handsome that you are too shy to talk.

(PRECIOUS bursts into laughter.)

CARL: I knew I could do it.

PRECIOUS: Do what?

CARL: Make you smile. So are you going to give me your number or going to keep acting stuck up?

SCENE 9:

AMELIN: Is it true?

PRECIOUS: Is what true?

AMELIN: That you and Carl is dating.

PRECIOUS: Kinda.

AMELIN: Kinda? Really, are you seriously going to lie in my face?

PRECIOUS: Okay, since you asked yes, yes we are.

AMELIN: Aw, I'm so happy for you.

PRECIOUS: Yeah me too.

AMELIN: No really.

CARL: Hey girls. Amelin can I steal her real fast?

AMELIN: She's all yours.

PRECIOUS: Hey wassup?

CARL: Nothing, I just missed you.

PRECIOUS: Really, already?

CARL: Yes already.

PRECIOUS: Aww. As much as I want to stay I have to get to class.

CARL: Walk you?

PRECIOUS: SURE.

SCENE 10:

MOTHER: I made dinner.

PRECIOUS: Okay and?

MOTHER: And? I want you to come eat at the dinner table and talk like we used to.

PRECIOUS: "Talk"? We haven't talked since Dad left, why you want to talk now?

MOTHER: Are you really going to act like this? Let it go.

PRECIOUS: Let what go? That you're a completely different person since dad left or that you don't think of no one but yourself? Pick one.

MOTHER: I'm trying, Precious.

PRECIOUS: Well, try harder.

SCENE 11:

(PRECIOUS is getting ready for school, as soon as she's done she will be on her way to school.)

AMELIN: I feel really bad about doing this to Precious, I mean what if she finds out? If someone tells her, or what if she see us...

CARL: Shaa, you talk way too much. (CARL pulls AMELIN closer.) Don't feel bad (Kiss) she's not going to find out (Kiss) most of all nobody's going to tell her. (Kiss) Besides I always had my eyes on you, I just didn't know how to talk or ask you. If anything happens I got you, plus I'll pick you over her any day. You're my love.

AMELIN: But I feel so bad.

PRECIOUS: About what?

To be continued...

About YPT

Young Playwrights' Theater (YPT) is the only professional theater in Washington, DC dedicated entirely to arts education. Our mission is to inspire young people to realize the power of their own voices. By teaching students to express themselves through the art of playwriting, YPT develops students' language skills, and empowers them with the creativity, confidence and critical thinking skills they need to succeed in school and beyond. YPT honors its students by involving them in a high-quality artistic process where they feel simultaneously respected and challenged and by engaging professional theater artists in producing student plays for the community.

YPT's Guiding Principles and Beliefs

Each student has a story worth telling. We believe the stories that our students have to tell are valuable and provide communities with a powerful perspective about the youth experience. The YPT process invites students to share their ideas, dreams and beliefs through the playwright's craft.

The arts are critical to excellence in education. We believe that theater and the art of playwriting are powerful tools in developing creativity and self-expression and in fostering learning across disciplines.

The process is more important than the product. We involve students in an ongoing creative process that enhances their learning and literacy while providing them with appropriate building blocks to construct a play. While we strive for artistic excellence, we believe the effect of the YPT process is ultimately more important than the work produced.

We strive for high standards from all who participate in our programs. The YPT process honors and respects the value of the work of its professional artists, students and partners. YPT expects the same self-discipline and respect from students as it does from the professionals involved in the process.

We meet students where they are. By reaching out to students through organized in-school, after-school and summer programs at neighborhood schools and community centers, YPT provides students of diverse backgrounds with a supportive environment where they can exchange ideas and express themselves freely.

Young Playwrights' Theater
Brigitte Pribnow Moore, Executive Director
Nicole Jost, Artistic Director
Karen Zacarías, Founding Artistic Director

2437 15th Street NW
Washington, DC 20009
(202) 387-9173
www.yptdc.org

www.ingramcontent.com/pod-product-compliance
Lightning Source LLC
Chambersburg PA
CBHW081149090426
42736CB00017B/3248